Letters from Jerusalem

The author, Eunice Holliday

Letters from Jerusalem

During the Palestine Mandate

Eunice Holliday

edited by John Holliday

Radcliffe Press
London • New York

Published in 1997 by
The Radcliffe Press
Victoria House
Bloomsbury Square
London
WC1B 4DZ

In the United States of America
and Canada, distributed by
St Martin's Press
175 Fifth Avenue
New York
NY 10010

A full CIP record of this book is available from
the British Library and the Library of Congress

ISBN 1 86064 085 0

Typeset and designed by Dexter Haven, London
Printed in Great Britain by WBC Ltd, Bridgend, Mid Glamorgan

To Eunice and Cliff Holliday

Contents

		page
List of Pictures		ix
Acknowledgements		xi
Maps		xii
Eunice's handwriting		xiv
1	Introduction	1
2	Jerusalem in 1922	3
3	1922	6
4	1923	18
5	1924	36
6	1925	51
7	1926	57
8	1927	71
9	1928	80
10	1929	96
11	1930	109
12	1931	124
13	1932	129
14	1933	138
15	1934	153
16	1935	166
Epilogue		170
Notes on the text		171
Short bibliography		172
Index		173

List of Pictures

		page
1	Eunice Holliday	ii
2	General Allenby at the taking of Jerusalem, Jaffa Gate	3
3	The Holy Sepulchre	7
4	The Dome of the Rock	8
5	Street of the Chains, Jerusalem	10
6	The Garden of Gethsemene and the Mount of Olives	12
7	Pottery in the old city	16
8	Eunice with Paul	33
9	Cliff with Paul	33
10	The Street of the Prophets	41
11	The Street of the Prophets	42
12	Beit Syriac	42
13	Beit Syriac	42
14	The offending Turkish clock tower over the Jaffa Gate	49
15	Lowering the tombstone of the crusader Philip d'Aubigny outside the Holy Sepulchre	58
16	Cliff at the tomb of Philip d'Aubigny	59
17	Eunice with Paul	62
18	Left to right: David and Alice Bomberg, Ben Dor, unknown, Paul, Harmat, Eunice	62
19	Jerusalem, looking towards the Holy Sepulchre, oil by David Bomberg, 1925	63
20	Wadi Kelt	67
21	At Wadi Kelt, left to right: Elizabeth, Cliff, Eunice, Douglas Broadbent(?), Harmat, Ben Dor	68
22	The Jericho-Jerusalem road	68
23	Father Tepper with Paul and John at Tabgha	84
24	The Hospice at Tabgha	85

25	At Capernaum	91
26	Sebastieh	92
27	The Wailing Wall	101
28	Army and police at the Damascus Gate during the 1929 riots	102
29	Army and police at Bethlehem during the 1929 riots	102
30	Bethlehem market	111
31	Beit Nassar, near Bethlehem	112
32	Beit Nassar, near Bethlehem	112
33	Outside the house: Eunice (back), Paul, John, Timothy, Ellie and a friend	113
34	Tan Tur Hospice	113
35	Eunice outside her cave at Petra	116
36	Petra	116
37	Petra	117
38	The Scottish Memorial Church	122
39	Cliff and Paul at the site of the Ethiopian Church on the Jordan	146
40	King David Hotel, Jerusalem	146
41	Family at Jaffa	155
42	At the German Hospice, Haifa	155
43	Haifa	156
44	Model of Kingsway, Haifa	156
45	The house in the German Colony	161
46	A coal delivery camel; the house in the German Colony	161
47	Paul, John, Timothy and Robin; the house in the German Colony	162
48	The family with Eunice's mother and father at their home in Birkdale	169

Acknowledgements

I am very grateful to my wife, Moira, for all the help that she has given me in the preparation of this book.

I am also gateful to Mrs Marjorie Drakeford and Dr Lester Crook for their early encouragement.

John Holliday
September 1996

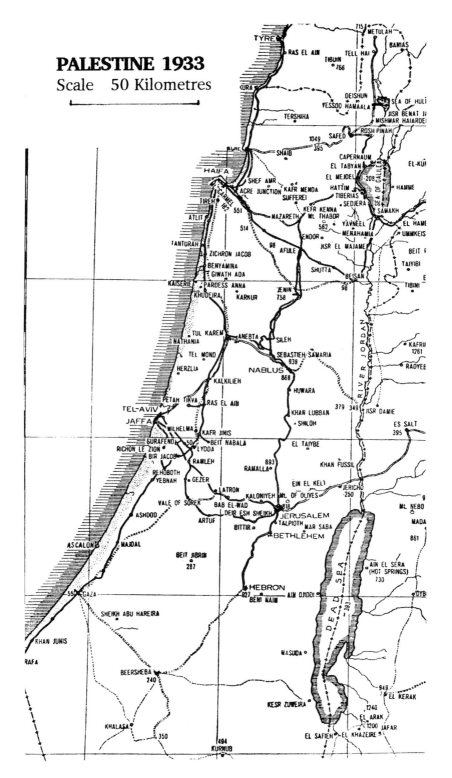

PALESTINE 1933
Scale   50 Kilometres

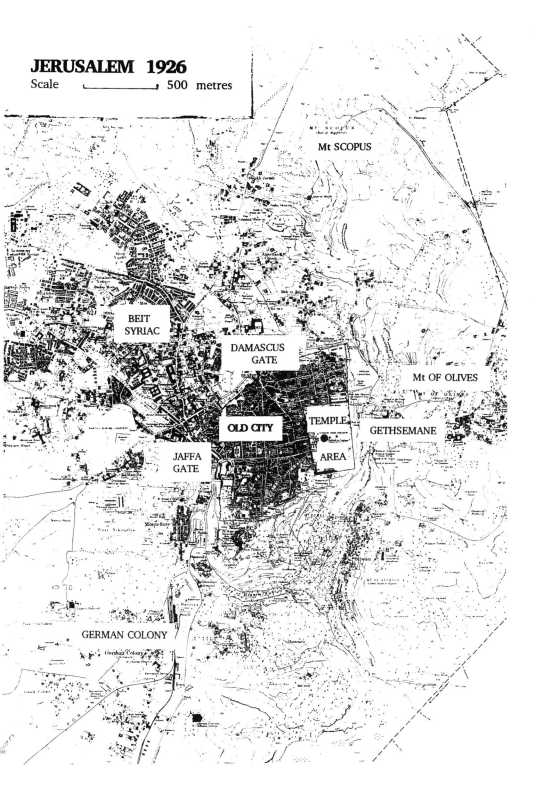

JERUSALEM 1926

Scale ⌞_____⌟ 500 metres

Mt SCOPUS

BEIT
SYRIAC

DAMASCUS
GATE

Mt OF OLIVES

OLD CITY

TEMPLE

GETHSEMANE

JAFFA
GATE

AREA

GERMAN COLONY

St. of Prophets
Jerusalem.
March 19th 1928

Dear Mother,

I wish you could have come with us yesterday, we went a picnic to a most lovely place about an hours car ride from here. It was a very green valley with a stream and flat rocks and on each side were grass fields covered with bright red anemones and pale pink cyclamen. It is a perfect place in the spring and it is

xiv

Letters from Jerusalem

1

Introduction

T he letters in this book were almost all written by Eunice Holliday to her
mother and father in Birkdale, Southport, and to her older sisters Elizabeth
and Lill; there are also a few written home by Elizabeth when she visited
Jerusalem.

Eunice's mother and father, Polly and Joshua Blackwell, were radical and
non-conformist in their outlook, church going and bringing their three daughters up to believe in socialism and freedom for women. One of their neighbours
and friends were the parents of A.J.P. Taylor, who says in his autobiography[1]:

> Joshua Blackwell and his family did not care about money at all. They lived
> in a small house, had no domestic servants and yet were happier than anyone
> else I knew… The Blackwells were the only literary family I knew. Their
> house was full of books… Joshua Blackwell wanted to build the new
> Jerusalem at home. He was the first person from whom I heard the words
> Revolution and Socialism.

The girls were encouraged to go to university and two of them went to Liverpool,
Elizabeth to take a degree in biology, Eunice to study architecture. It was there
that she met her future husband Cliff, also studying architecture. Cliff came
from a more conventional Yorkshire family near Leeds, but, like Eunice, was
unconventional, and their outlook on life had much in common.

On qualification, Cliff worked for a short while for Professor Patrick
Abercrombie at Liverpool, and so began a relationship in work, and as a friend,
which lasted much of his life. I surmise that it was through the help and
encouragement of Abercrombie that Cliff got the post of Civic Advisor to the
City of Jerusalem, where architecture and planning were given a high priority by
Ronald Storrs, then Military Governor of the City. Cliff was 24, Eunice only 22
when they went out.

The letters were kept by Eunice's family, and in later years she selected from
them and typed out these extracts. I have read almost all the originals – a few are
missing – and I have added a few paragraphs, and omitted quite a lot about the
children, clothes, presents from England, illnesses and other domestic details of

the time. What is contained here about the country, its people and customs, architecture and history is, I hope, a useful commentary of life in Palestine during the British Mandate.

At the beginning of each year I have added a small commentary.

2

Jerusalem in 1922

C ities take on an image which grows from their people, historical events, buildings and landscape. Nowhere has this been stronger in the Western World than in Jerusalem. The events concerning Jesus and the origins of Christianity, the old city and its walls, the Garden of Gethsemene and the Mount of Olives: all these and the very culture of Western Europe, conjure up images which may be fanciful but are nevertheless powerful.

General Allenby at the taking of Jerusalem, Jaffa Gate

In 1917, when the British captured the City from the Turks, and when the Jews had been given the promise of their homeland, the feelings of millions must have been heightened. The reality was rather different. There had been centuries of neglect and poverty in the old city, with the introduction of many unsympathetic buildings. To the west and north, sporadic building had developed along the roads and between, providing a newer and often unattractive Jerusalem, much of it comprising new Jewish settlements from the late nineteenth century. German and Greek colonies were built to the south west, but south and east of the city, the Hinnom and Kidron valleys, bounding the site of the old city of David with the Mount of Olives, were relatively unspoilt. The population was about 70,000.

The landscape is hilly, and the city lies at about 750 metres above the Mediterranean Sea. Only 20 kilometres to the east lies the Dead Sea, 397 metres below sea level and visible from the Mount of Olives. Summers were hot, winters cool and water scarce. The supply for Jerusalem had always come from pools, cisterns and wells, augmented in Solomon's time by pools to the south near Bethlehem. As well as shortages of water, there was no electricity. The land was heavily eroded and stony; olive was the most common tree, and wild flowers were abundant. Camels and donkeys provided more transport than motor vehicles.

Politically, the British had taken over an insoluble problem, having promised, with the Balfour Declaration, a homeland for the Jews in a country dominated by Arabs. The declaration of November 1917 stated:

His Majesty's Government view with favour the establishment in Palestine of a National Home for the Jewish People, and will use their best endeavours to facilitate the achievement of that object, it being understood that nothing shall be done which may prejudice the civil and religious rights of existing non-Jewish communities in Palestine, or the rights and political status enjoyed by the Jews in any other country.

The Declaration was endorsed by the principal Allied Powers and embodied in the Treaty of Sèvres signed on 10 August 1920. In that treaty, under which Turkey renounced her sovereignty over Palestine, it was provided that the country should be entrusted to a Mandatory Power. As for the holy places, the doctrine of the status quo was declared, and all historic rights protected.

The intent was to try and balance the conflicting demands, but these could not be met, particularly as promises had been made to the Arabs during the war, but without the sanction of the British Government. A sense of injustice, along with the scale and rate of Jewish immigration, lay at the heart of the interwar disturbances.

The military authorities had been quick to act on the conservation, planning and control of the City. Plans by W.H. McLean, in 1918, and Patrick Geddes, in 1919, protected the open land to the south and east, and the views of the old city, while providing for new development north and west. In addition, Ronald Storrs, the Military Governor, had issued an order prohibiting the demolition, erection, alteration or repair of any buildings within a radius of 2500 metres of the Damascus Gate, without a permit from the Governor. C.R. Ashbee was appointed the first Civic Advisor. As a leader of the British Arts and Crafts Movement, he devoted his energies to re-establishing ancient crafts such as pottery, started conservation work on the walls and gates, and was secretary to the Pro-Jerusalem Society which was founded by Ronald Storrs in 1918. It was to this post that Clifford Holliday succeeded in 1922 and, as an architect and town planner, extended this detailed work to the wider task of town planning.

These early letters home give first impressions: of the old city, the Holy Sepulchre and the Dome of the Rock; walks outside the walls, of the Arabs and their customs, many confirming images derived from the Bible. They also give a picture of domestic life: house hunting, servants, shopping and friends. It must have been a period of great hope, tempered by the riots which had already taken place and by the knowledge that the political forces which caused them were likely to grow. For the present, however, Jerusalem was a place of exciting expectations.

3

1922

About the first thing I saw, Mother, at Port Said was a large sky sign proclaiming 'Dewar's Whisky' followed by two smaller ones of Pear's Soap and Lipton's Tea. So you see I felt quite at home at once.

27th August

Professor and Mrs Garstang put us up when we first arrived in Jerusalem. This is an old Moslem house, really very big but the whole of the ground floor is given up to the School of Archaeology. The second floor is therefore the dwelling part, and you can enter it from the courtyard outside by a flight of steps up the side of the house, onto a verandah (we had dinner there one night under the stars, it was beautiful). The door from outside leads to a huge hall with doors on each side; the rooms have stone floors, whitewashed walls but elaborately painted ceilings. The third floor of the house is one huge room, with big windows all round: it is divided into two by a partition, half is our bedroom and half Meroe's nursery (Meroe is their little daughter of six). She is teaching me Arabic, throwing a whole series of nouns at me haphazardly. The easiest is mish-mish, an apricot. Before 8.30 I am downstairs drawing and Cliff is at the Governorate. Isn't it queer that I should be helping excavations when I have been wanting to go digging for such a long time? I am drawing out the plan of the chief building at Askalon (*an ancient city on the coast*). I draw till eleven when we have little lunch in the garden, then I draw again until proper lunch at one.

On Saturday Cliff and I went to have dinner with Colonel Storrs, who is the Governor. He has the most beautiful house, and hundreds of wonderful things in it. (Cliff has met Sir Herbert Samuel, the High Commissioner, too). He goes riding on a horse very morning to get to know the place. He is getting on well and takes over from Ashbee on the 1st September. He took me to the Citadel, the old medieval fortress at the Jaffa Gate.

The Church of the Holy Sepulchre is the most wonderful and gorgeous place I have ever seen. Of course it seems frightfully complicated when you first see it. There is the main part which contains the tomb: this we could not see as it was full of people; then there are different chapels for the Greek church, Latin church, Armenian church and heaps more, and hundreds of little altars and

The Holy Sepulchre

shrines marking special places, each with some particular significance. It is rather difficult, at first, to understand how the place of the tomb and the place of the cross and all the other historic spots can be enclosed in the one building, but the building so surrounds the whole district that it is on different levels, and by leaving the tomb and mounting a lot of steps to the place of the cross you are really mounting what was Mount Calvary. Nothing is missing: just as you go in, there is the slab of stone on which Christ's body was embalmed, and a light a few yards away marks the place where the Marys stood and watched. The slab is surrounded by candles: don't think I mean the little white things Elsie reads by in bed, but imagine something nearly a foot in diameter and at least ten feet high.

6th September

We have been house hunting, but it has turned out to be a rather difficult business. There is a great shortage of decent houses and, ten-to-one, if you do find one, the landlord can't speak a word of English. We got a funny old Jew, who is a sort of house agent, to keep a look out for us but people have such impossible ideas about light and sanitation and cleanliness that they aren't very much use.

It is now Friday morning at 9.30, and I have already been to the shops and back. I shop in the Jaffa Road, just outside the Jaffa Gate, as all the people there can speak a little English, but it would be impossible to go bargaining in Arabic in the old city. So far it's all right, as there are decent grocery shops in the Jaffa Road, but all the vegetables and fruit etc, are sold in the Arab markets. Do you know mosquitoes don't seem to like me; Cliff has been bitten quite often. That's the best of having a thick skin.

I have never told you about the Dome of the Rock: we went to see it last Sunday. It is in a very crowded part of the old city, the Jewish Quarter is on one side. It stands high on a huge open space which has arcades running along two sides and odd little archways and bits of building, all in the beautiful pinky stone which is also used for paving the whole square. The very clean stone against the bright sky looked wonderful. The mosque itself stands in the centre and is being restored with beautiful blue and green tiles. There is a little domed open building at one side which is supposed to have been built on the spot where a chain hung from Heaven in the days of Solomon, and acted as a sort of judge. If two people were having an argument they went to the chain, which would swing towards the one who was in the right. Of course we had to take off our shoes at the door of the mosque. The inside I don't like as well as the outside: it is so dark in comparison to the bright light that you don't get the full effect of all the gold and coloured mosaic.

The Dome of the Rock

12th September

I must tell you about the American Colony. A good many years ago, a small religious sect came from America to Jerusalem to await the end of the world. On the appointed day they all went up to the Mount of Olives and waited – nothing happened – so they tried again the next week, or month, or year: still nothing happened. Not having any money, they set to work to earn some, and now they are quite a big colony, all living on a sort of communal principle. They have a huge store in the town, a lace industry for the poor and an orphanage. Mrs Whiting is an important member of the colony, and is the treasurer of the Pro-Jerusalem Society. I had tea there with heaps of other ladies: one of them is going to have a baby next month so I told her I was having one too, and she said she would help me. The Government Hospital has just opened a new maternity hospital which is run by a Miss Ingham.

Prof. and Mrs Garstang came home on Monday to attend the ceremony at Government House, when Lord Allenby came and the High Commissioner was sworn in. There was great excitement, troops in the Citadel and marching around the town with bands. It was funny to see the dignified Selem (Prof.'s main servant) running down the road to see the soldiers. I am sure you will be pleased to know that I was introduced to Allenby. On Tuesday morning, he came to visit the School of Archaeology and so, of course, came to see the drawings of Askalon, and I had to expound upon columns etc. He is a most imposing individual, of hugest size; he was in civvies, but he must look fine in khaki I should think.

We have got a house! A really marvellous house too – Beit Gebshi on Mount Scopus. It is a quiet new and very small flat, consisting of two bedrooms, kitchen, sitting room and infinitesimal bathroom and shower! This is fine for Jerusalem, as most people have to put in their own baths et cetera. Through the sitting room windows there is a fine view of the Mount of Olives, and another of the city. We have no garden, as we are not on the ground floor but we have a flat roof to sit out on moonlit evenings.

I must describe to you my expeditions to the market with Selem to buy kitchen utensils and groceries. Selem goes along in front with a large basket and I follow behind until we get to the shops, then I point out things I want and Selem bargains in Arabic. When we get a basketful we hire a small boy, who carries it on his head until we get out of the City, where we hire a cab to take us home.

Tell Lill to put on the Arabic gramophone record and she can imagine me preparing lunch and listening to the painters singing outside. The people are awfully fond of gramophones, the kind with the large green or red horns, and all the prosperous-looking Moslems come to their cafes and sit on little stools smoking hookahs. The landlord lives in the flat below. He was very relieved to find we were married, and not brother and sister. Our landlord is a Moslem, and can't speak any English, but next door there is a maid, a native of Nazareth, who can speak English, so we fetch her to act as interpreter.

I have got a maid! She is Russian and can only speak a very little English, but knows some Arabic. I'm rather lucky because good maids are not easy to get here, and the Russians have the reputation of being very good workers and exceptionally clean; my one has the most beautiful teeth and fresh complexion, if that is anything to go by. Anyway, she will cook, keep clean the whole house, do the shopping, iron and wash the small things: to use her own words, she will be responsible for the whole house. She asked me if we wanted our morning tea at five, so that she must get up early.

Street of the Chains, Jerusalem

The milkman comes round every morning at seven and he sells eggs; then there is a bread and cake man who arrives about eleven; and today the dustman came: he comes every morning too because, you see, there are no fires and no dustbins here, and you collect your rubbish in a tin. Eggs here (quite big ones) are ten for a shilling, and we get six huge bunches of grapes for five pence and about twenty tomatoes for five pence. Bread too is cheaper than at Mossley Hill.

Last Sunday we went to Colonel Storrs to tea: there were five men and one lady besides us, all Jews except one. On Monday we went to dinner to a Mr Bentwich, the Attorney General: he has very a swagger house in the German

Colony, about three miles from our house, so we had to go in a gharry (what we call a Victoria) the only kind of cab here. It was fun driving in the dark with all the stars shining. We met the son (Edwin or 'Nebi') and daughter-in-law of Sir Herbert Samuel: they brought us home in their car.

25th September

Today was Meroe's birthday and we went to her party, a joint one with Joanna Grant, the small daughter of General Grant, who is Head of the Public Works Department. When we arrived, about thirty small children were having tea in the big hall, Meroe at one end of the long table and Joanna at the other.

I must tell you about the Bristol Gardens: it is the best known cafe in Jerusalem at the back of the Jaffa Road. It is just a garden with lots of trees and a fountain and little tables and lights and an orchestra of varied music, including ragtime. It's really quite exciting and un-Jerusalem-like. When we are thirsty, we go there and drink ginger beer in the middle of our shopping.

Well, my maid has arrived: she is called Martha (pronounced Marta) and so far is excellent. She prepared us a very good lunch and dinner with very little instruction from me, because we can't say much to each other. But I said 'pudding' and we had a beautiful custard with caramel sauce. You can make omelettes and souffles ten times lighter here than at home: I wonder why?

29th September

Yesterday I went to Government Hospital to see Mrs Ingham, but found that she had gone away for three weeks, so I saw the assistant matron, Miss Gibb: she herself is a qualified midwife. I saw the private wards: nice little white rooms, they look quite comfy. 50 piastres (10/-) a day. I'm frightfully excited about Elsie (Eunice's eldest sister) coming at Easter – it will be splendid – and perhaps father? Why not all come? Martha is still very satisfactory. She does everything without being told anything. This morning we bought two small chickens for three shillings and sixpence: they are alive and sitting in a corner of the kitchen. I wonder if Martha is going to kill them?

By the way, people never dream of making a plan before they build a house! They just begin and hope for the best; it's worked out like a kind of puzzle as they go along. If they put up a wall, and it turns out to be in the wrong place, they just take it down again. They made a very small bathroom and then very gaily bought a huge bath, shower and geyser. Well of course there is scarcely room for the bath, so the geyser goes in the kitchen.

You will be wondering what we are doing about furniture. We have three of Mr Ashbee's chairs: we are painting them red and black; we had a small dining table made of plain wood, which we are painting to match; then we have bought three wicker chairs for comfort. The American Colony sold us four sets of shelves, rather dirty and rickety, which we have patched up, two in the kitchen and two as sideboard and bookcase. The floors are covered with an elaborate pattern of tiles; we have Ashbee's rug.

7th October

We have found a walk with a most gorgeous view just near to our house. It is up our end of the Mount of Olives, which is a long hill and stretches for quite a long way. We found it going to see the British War Cemetery, which is at the top. There are two kinds of crosses, Christian and Jewish, but it is rather incongruous to see a Christian cross over the grave of a Turkish prisoner. It was dreadful to see a cross with no name, just 'Unknown British Soldier' or sometimes just 'Unknown'. When we walked up the road a little higher than the cemetery, we came to the most wonderful view of the hills of Judea and the Jordan Valley. We overlooked the part where the Jordan enters the Dead Sea. It was really like our picture at home. I felt just like Moses. But the colours were wonderful. It was just sunset, and the mountains were bright pink. We sat on the roof last night and watched the stars come out: the roof isn't finished yet, but I had a deck chair amongst the debris. I wish you could see the evening star.

20th October

When we arrived, everything was in a most hopeless muddle. Cliff found the Pro-Jerusalem Society about bankrupt and all the members fed up to the teeth. Professor Garstang, who is really a most sensible matter-of-fact business-like person, told Cliff all about everything, and I believe the first meeting was a great

The Garden of Gethsemene and the Mount of Olives

success. When it comes to town planning, no-one here, not even Storrs, knows the first thing about civic design, and everything is done in the most haphazard way. For instance, the Mayor has a passion for making big new roads, so he suggests a route cutting through anywhere, utterly regardless of what may come in the way of it. Only the other day, Cliff was taken to see a very poor old Jew whose house stood in the way of one of the new roads, and was going to be knocked down, and he had nowhere else to live. And they never seem to dream of giving anyone compensation.

A letter from Cliff dated 21 October lists his work as: a town planning scheme for Jerusalem, first stage collecting data. Tree planting. Work on the Citadel and city wall. The encouragement of arts and crafts and lastly building permits.

Mr and Mrs Blake, our neighbours, are leaving, and the landlord invited them and us to tea at four o'clock. I must describe it all to you from the beginning. To start with, a Moslem's house always has one room near the front with a separate door. Here the man of the house can entertain his friends without fear of them seeing his wives. Into this room, therefore, we were taken. It was white-washed and spotlessly clean, with lots of windows with cream curtains and plants on the sills. All round the room, in a row, on three sides were chairs looking rather like Victorian red plush ones, only these were all covered with white linen coats and looked just exactly like dentist's chairs. In the centre of the room was a round table covered with a big white cloth, and on the table were dishes piled high with the most exciting party biscuits. There were four glass dishes of the biggest and most rosy apples you can imagine, plates of bananas and little plates piled with chocolate. On a side table was tea and two cakes with a diameter of at least a foot, not to mention four dishes of Arab cakes and a plate of sandwiches. Well, we felt we must do justice to the feast, but I must say I felt a little overwhelmed, and have partaken of a sandwich, two cakes, a biscuit, an apple and a banana (carefully peeled and handed to me naked by our host). I felt I didn't want another meal for some time. Mrs Blake took her children to see the landlord's wife, so I went too. We all sat in a big circle: Cliff and Mr Blake stayed behind.

Cliff says Askalon is beautiful, palm trees and banana and orange trees and a beautiful shore and cliffs and little mud villages. He heard jackals crying in the night, and this morning bathed in the Mediterranean.

I had two visitors this afternoon. First came Mrs Deedes, who is either mother or sister to Sir William Deedes, I don't know which. She is a very nice old lady, and was very pleased with our house! The other visitors were Mr and Mrs Home, wanting information about how to get furniture et cetera. It seems ridiculous that we have only been here about six weeks, and can already advise people about cheap places for shopping.

27th October

Last night it rained for the first time, and in the morning the trees looked beautifully fresh green. It was still cloudy and dull, so we decided to go to the Garden of Gethsemene, which is about an hour's walk from our house, and I couldn't have done it if the sun had been out. As it was we enjoyed the walk, in a valley of olive trees called the Valley of the Dead, because it is full of rock-cut tombs.

Of course there is no grass in the valley, just the red sandy soil, but we suddenly came across a whole clump of crocuses. I have pressed a crocus to send you: they had sprung up with the rain and looked so fresh, they are the first spring flowers we have seen. The Garden of Gethsemene is nice, very shady and peaceful, lots of trees and little paths, something like a small park. There is a very baroque little Russian church built in the middle of it, with gilt domes; a Russian sister showed us inside but it was rather tawdry and disappointing; the outside was the best. Just outside is the tomb of the Virgin. We went inside, and a Greek priest took us over, down a huge flight of steps, right under the earth into a big square room, all dark so we had candles. The roof is strung with rows and rows of little lamps and glass balls like Christmas tree decorations, little rooms lead off big ones. There is the Virgin's tomb, Joseph's tomb, Mary's parents' tomb et cetera. The bodies are supposed to have been brought here some time centuries ago.

We had great fun with Martha about the census: we just managed to get her surname, because she had to write it down and her English writing is slightly difficult to read. The question of whether married or single was most difficult: we didn't know whether she was married or not and she didn't know what married meant, so we felt pretty hopeless. We settled it by pointing at me and saying 'madame', to Cliff 'monsieur' and to Martha saying 'mademoiselle'. Then she said 'Iwa, iwa' (which is Arabic for 'Yes, yes'). We did ages the same way. I said 'Madame 22, Martha?' She is 32.

I like the Arabs very much indeed, they seem so much more dignified, refined and well bred than either Jews or Europeans: somehow they seem so grand, as if they come of a very great people, and yet they are so simple. We have some new English people come to live in the flat below, the Homes. I went one morning to see if they wanted any assistance and found an officer bossing the landlord about in the most disgusting manner, calling him Mahomet and Mahmoud and all sorts of names. If I had been the landlord, I would have thrown something at him.

10th November

Cliff has bought me a lovely thing for a present. It is a garment called a burnous, made of two pieces of material joined at the sides with holes left at the top for arms, and split up the front. English ladies wear them for evening wraps or dressing gowns. You can get them in beautiful silk of most gorgeous colours. Mine is champagne colour embroidered with gold and in Damascus silk. People say it will wash and wear for ever. The Bedouin Arabs all wear the exact same garment only in thick material and usually brown and fawn stripes, or blue. They look beautiful, tramping along by their camels; their headdress is a big square of striped cotton or silk, edged with tassels held onto the head by the typical two black bands of wool. They have their burnous wide open, and it flies behind them as they walk.

The Garstangs leave tomorrow. I have been very busy drawing Askalon for the last few weeks, as the Professor wanted all the drawings worked out so he could take them with him. I haven't had time to ink them in or finish them off in any way, but that can be done in Liverpool. One drawing he is leaving for me to finish: after that I must turn to sewing.

We had rain last night, heavy rain with thunder, and since then it has been cooler. Cliff has a funny job: he has been asked to design an inscription to have the signatures of all the government officials complementing Sir Herbert and Lady Samuel on their silver wedding.

It was Mr Home's birthday, so we celebrated by going a picnic up Mount Scopus. We had our tea at the top of a hill overlooking the Dead Sea and the Jordan Valley. It was beautiful. After tea, we walked over the hills: we have a new occupation, that is hunting for flints of the stone men. Mr Home has quite a collection, so he taught us what to look for. Mr Home took Cliff to the Jordan: he is superintending a new bridge there. I can't travel in a car, at least people won't let me: they say it's too bumpy. I shall have to wait until next year before I see other places. I shall miss Bethlehem on Christmas Eve: it is the custom to go to the midnight mass at the Church of the Nativity and see all the ceremonies. I shall see them next year.

I must tell you a rather nice story I heard the other day. It seems that last week an old sheik was robbed by bandits on the Jaffa Road. He was found, and taken to the nearest hospital. When he asked if his relations could visit him, they told him between 3 and 5 o'clock in the afternoons. Behold, next day a huge crowd of people streamed into the hospital garden and encamped there; they had milk, chickens and other provisioning to last them weeks. The whole of the sheik's village had turned out to condole!

Cliff took me, the other day, to see some potteries. An ancient industry has been revived by the Pro-Jerusalem Society, and is in quite a flourishing condition now. It turns out rather beautiful bowls, jars, vases etc, rather coarse make, but very attractive. We saw the vases being shaped from clay, then rows of pots before and after baking. Small boys draw the designs, girls colour them, and finally we saw the big kiln where they are finished off, and all being done in the queerest

Pottery in the old city

little rooms right in the middle of the old city. We also saw what is known as the Jerusalem looms, where materials are hand made. This industry is not so successful as the potteries, but they have some stuffs which are good and some wonderful hand-made towels.

All the streets in the old city are being taken up, and pipes laid down, to carry government water to the public taps. And new taps are being put up; you see so many of the poor people have to fetch their water, just as they used to draw it from wells in the Bible. It's queer to see the old water jars being superseded by petrol tins. I must tell you about petrol tins, they are absolutely numberless and put to all sorts of uses. Innumerable articles are made out of them; lamps, water jars, jugs, cake and roasting tins, dust pans etc. And in their usual shape, when they are known as 'tenekies' they are used for collecting rubbish (we have one which a man empties each day) or carrying water to plants.

1st December

Well winter has come at last: it started quite suddenly on Tuesday night with a most violent wind, dust was blowing all over the place. On Wednesday morning Cliff said, 'When this wind drops it will rain' and it was so. It's rained ever since. It's perfectly miraculous how these two days of rain have made all the little grass

16

shoots grow: there is a sort of green carpet coming up all over the brown earth. We have a little stove that keeps us so warm in the evenings.

I was in the suq the other day with Mrs Home, where they sell materials. We stopped at one shop which had piles of rather nice cottons. We asked where they came from and they said, 'Manchester'. Oranges are beginning – we have had our first this week – Jaffas of course. I bought six for two piastres (five pence). We discovered the other day that we can buy ripping Turkish delight from the man down the road for two piastres a pound. Then yesterday, we bought some halva: this is native food made of sesame, it looks like a kind of solid honey.

9th December
Tomorrow is the anniversary of the British entry into Palestine, and we have to celebrate. There is a church service in the morning which I believe is going to be rather queer, a mixed ceremony.

4

1923

The birth of Paul, the first son, marks the start of 1923, and the experiences of maternity and hospital far removed from England. But the event was a happy one, with the warmth and friendliness of those around. Eunice and Cliff found the often exotic and exciting life of Jerusalem much preferable to what appeared, at that distance, to be a dull existence in England. Cliff, in particular, wrote to this effect in a letter which is not published here.

Nevertheless, there must have been strains. Housing was difficult: it was rented, and Arab landlords evidently expected people to move on, if not every year, pretty frequently. A first child is always a concern, and it is not surprising that Eunice's mother expressed it. Palestine must have seemed very far away. The sea trip took ten days, air services were yet to begin, and there was no telephone. Eunice's father and mother wrote of 'Arabs with daggers waiting round corners'. They were not, but there were incidents, and I remember as a child being frightened by the possibilities. The carrying of daggers was a traditional custom of the Arabs.

There was also the threat of general disturbances arising from tension between Arabs and Jews over the immigration of Jews and their buying of land, or specific quarrels over sites. The Wailing Wall, the only remaining part of the Old Temple area, was a continual source of argument, and a trigger for disturbances. There had been riots in Jerusalem in 1920 and in Jaffa in 1921. Easter was always a potentially difficult time, with the Christian and Jewish festivals coming together, and with the Arab Nebi Musa procession taking place. Nebi Musa, described by Eunice in this year's letters, involved a procession to the tomb of Moses (Nebi Musa) near Jericho and then up to Jerusalem.

The feast and fast of Ramadan, as well as a visit to a village wedding, are also described. The wedding, in particular, gives a graphic account of traditional life; and the way in which Cliff and Eunice mixed with both Arab and Jew is evident from the time they arrived in Jerusalem. Another newcomer, David Bomberg, the painter, and his wife Alice are introduced in this year: Bomberg was to paint a large number of views in and around the City over the next few years, and eventually to become an internationally renowned painter.

Eunice's sister Elizabeth was to visit Jerusalem four times over the years. Elizabeth was the eldest of the three sisters, a botanist who was a lecturer at Royal

Holloway College in the University of London. In this first trip, she describes a trip taken by the whole family to the Lebanon and Syria. Perhaps it was made because Cliff and Eunice thought they might be leaving the country after the end of a two year contract. There was obviously some expectancy that this might be so, in view of a letter the following year saying that they had decided to renew the contract. Already, this year, Cliff started work on a first ever town planning survey of Jerusalem, and he no doubt wanted to finish a town plan.

This year closes with a visit to the Church of the Nativity in Bethlehem, which was built over the supposed birthplace of Jesus. The holy places were, on the whole, taken at face value by Eunice, as fitting the stories of the Bible, although evidence is not conclusive. If there was doubt, it is not expressed in the letters, and the large amount of archaeological work that has taken place since then does not, on the whole, change the picture. Visitors now, as then, are probably told much the same story.

6th January

You will be surprised to hear we have sacked Martha. She got obstreperous, and when I told her to do things she just gabbled at me in Russian, which was most annoying, seeing I couldn't gabble back. I gave her a week's notice and she flew into a temper and was out of the house in about ten minutes. I haven't seen her since. I've discovered that she thought babies were 'mush nice', and was going in a month anyway. Of course, I should not have sacked her now if I hadn't got another to replace her. Mrs Blake's maid Sophie is coming to me: she is a Nazareth woman, a Christian and speaks English. Also, she likes babies and knows how to look after them, so she ought to be useful.

Do you know that we (and the Latin Church) are known as the Unorthodox Christians? The Orthodox Christians (Greeks, Russians, Abyssinians, Copts, et cetera) have their Christmas tomorrow. Their whole calendar is quite different to ours. But where Christmas is our great feast, they concentrate on Easter.

9th January

Storrs has gone on a two-month tour to America to collect money for the Pro-Jerusalem Society, so Cliff is working under the Assistant Governor Mr Luke. He finds him better to work with, but of course he hasn't got Storrs' fascinating personality.

Einstein is visiting Jerusalem. He gave a lecture last night which I think I should have gone to if I had been out of retirement, so to speak, if only to see him. I shouldn't have understood a word as he doesn't speak English. Relativity in English is bad enough, but relativity in French!

25th January

I'm spending most of my time at present sitting on the roof... I can see for miles. I watch all the cars going up and down to Government House, and all the peasants going down to the city with their chickens and eggs and camels, donkeys, cows et cetera. Not to mention six ducks and two turkeys that are promenading up and down the road.

You will like the little Hebron glass shop. The old man sits cross-legged on the floor of his little shop nearly buried in rows and rows of beads and strings of glass bracelets and all sorts of queer little glass things. I have a funny little pyramid charm of blue glass beads threaded on wire round a little piece of soda. They are put on babies to keep off the evil eye.

31st January

The much-needed rain has come at last, just in the nick of time. The water was coming to an end, and PWD² was beginning to arrange for water to be brought to Jerusalem by train. Anyway that won't be necessary now, it's poured for three days. You say in your letter it was blowing a hurricane, and do we have wind in Jerusalem? I expect your hurricane was a mild zephyr in comparison to the wild fury that is blowing at present here: it's really tremendous, it roars round the house and I expect pieces to fly off at any minute. Three tiles are off the roof already.

Last weekend was beautifully fine, and we went two walks exploring tombs: we are about in the middle of the valley, so on Saturday we walked left and on Sunday to the right. Sat's walk was more interesting from a botanical point of view: we found our first red anemones (the lilies of the field). The colour is wonderful, the most vivid scarlet you can possibly imagine. I believe in spring the whole country is covered with them, which is wonderful when you think of them at about three pence each at Dingley's. Other things we found were huge clumps of leaves, like very big lily of the valley leaves: Mr Home says they are asphodel, and in the caves we discovered maidenhair fern. On Sunday, we found some fine tombs: the whole valley is positively riddled with them. They are huge square chambers cut out of the solid rock, one room leading to another so that they go right under the earth: we found a fine stone sarcophagus in one of them. You enter most by little doors, but one we found had columns up the front and looked rather grand. Some we found harbouring dead goats instead of dead kings.

I'm beginning to understand the commandments. 'Thou shalt not covet thy neighbour's wife, nor his ox, nor his ass...' is quite comprehensible now. Wives here are not individuals, they are possessions. Sophie gives us all sorts of information about Moslem households. For instance, it's considered very unlucky to go up to anyone and admire their baby or their donkey: it may give them the evil eye... 'thou shalt not covet...'

This is supposed to be the land of milk and honey, but I've seen no honey yet, and milk and butter are two of the most expensive eatables.

13th February
The hospital, Jerusalem, telegram
Paul arrived safely. All well. Cliff.

15th February
From Cliff to Elizabeth
Paul is wonderful and beautiful. Our hearts are filled with joy. He is quite big, nearly eight pounds. I'm sure he smiled the first day: no-one believes this except us. He sleeps, sleeps, sleeps, awfully good and doesn't wake Eunice up in the night.

26th February
Today I am dressed, and am lying on a long chair in the garden; it's a glorious spring day... the garden here is – or has been – rather fine, you see the hospital used to be the Russian Consulate. Besides Miss Ingham and Miss Skieff, there are four other nurses here. Two, a Greek and a Syrian, speak English and look after me, the other two are Americans, and in charge of the big ward. Their names are Nurse Jameely (the Syrian) and Nurse Tespinna, the others are Rosa and Sultana. The ward outside my little room is for free patients, and was nearly full when I arrived. New babies were appearing every day, and such a variety: Arabs, Americans, Jews and a Negress. The babies are brought in to visit me, and they are such queer little specimens. They are all dressed in 'swaddling clothes' or something approaching that, a garment which consists of a square of material wrapped round them very tightly, keeping their arms and legs quite straight (these people are terrified of bow legs) so that they cannot move an inch. Some patients have never been in a bed before. Some only stay about three days and then insist on going home, and what kind of homes, I wonder?

I have had heaps of visitors: two are new acquaintances, Mrs Luke, wife of the Assistant Governor, and Mrs Grant, wife of the Director of Public Works. The first day I had flowers and a letter from Mrs Whiting, flowers from Mrs Samuel and such a nice letter from Mrs Deedes.

6th March
At visiting day at the hospital, I was watching the people when three Moslem women arrived; directly they saw me they were most interested, came right up and surrounded poor Paul, all jabbering away in Arabic. I was most annoyed, and waved them away, whereupon they sat on the floor about two yards off and started showering questions at me. It is quite impossible to stop these people by

saying you are English and don't know Arabic: they are unquenchable, so I sat solemnly eating an orange whilst they took in all my European peculiarities. In time I succeeded in having them removed – not before I had begun to feel like a monkey at the zoo – but in a few minutes a whole host of people bore down upon me and proceeded to gather around the cot for an inspection. The excitement was all because Paul is lying outside and they are all firmly convinced that he will die of cold; also, he has nothing over his face, which makes them more anxious still. The Arab women never take their babies out until they are five months old because they catch cold (in the heat!) and every time they cry they feed them. Not long ago they didn't bathe them until they were about four months.

I am going home on Friday; I feel very virtuous having been here so long. I shall have been here nearly a month. I shall not have any housework to do at home. Sophie seems to be running the house quite well by herself, and we have enlarged our domestic staff so that she can help me with Paul. The enlargement is a small boy from an orphanage. I join with Mrs Richmond: she has him from early morning until ten and I from ten to twelve. He scrubs floors, cleans brasses and silver and does all sorts of odd jobs.

2nd April
To Elizabeth

Mr Home says that Solomon's Pools are full of miles of algae, and he will be most pleased for you to clean them: he promises you two natives as helpers if you will undertake to clean out the pools. There is plenty of vegetation on Mount Carmel, and plenty of cacti in Jerusalem.

We have not seen very much of the Easter Celebration (thanks to Paul) but Cliff went to see the Holy Fire and was very much impressed: he came back saying it was the most pagan thing he had ever seen, and that Birkdale Congregation Church would have a fit if they knew that this was Orthodox Christianity.

I never told you about the Nebi Musa procession. Nebi Musa means Tomb of Moses, and every year Moslems have a procession to the tomb and stay there for a week, feasting and praying. We all went, Sophie pushing Paul, and armed with food for the day, and settled down in the Jewish cemetery, which is on the roadside. The procession was the queerest I have ever seen, a more disorganised affair you could not imagine, but then that is typical of the country. The people came along in batches, just a crowd with banners of silk, of all colours, then a crowd dancing – Arabic dancing is a joke – then a crowd singing and waving swords or sticks and, interspersed, groups of mounted police and soldiers to see there was no fighting. Quite the nicest part of the day was to see all the fellaheen (peasants from the villages) in their new clothes. The colours were wonderful, bright pink, purple or blue velvet coats, yellow dresses with embroideries in red and green et cetera, and all wore a white veil. It was a gorgeous sight: we saw a very tiny Arabic girl in a bright purple velvet coat and bonnet trimmed with pink roses and lace. The nicest thing was a very small, fat, brown piccaninny in a yellow coat and little red fez, carrying a large olive branch in one hand; I have never seen anything so funny, we laughed at him till we cried.

Father and mother were worried for our safety out here, and wrote of the Arabs with daggers waiting round corners, but I would just like to tell you that the only unpleasantness we have had was from two British soldiers drunk on our doorstep. This pleasant little episode happened while I was in hospital, and Cliff and Sophie had an exciting time. Cliff went out to stop them fighting and they began to fight him, so he retired, got a bucket of water and poured it on top of them from above. Then Sophie went to the camp to get them removed.

27th April

On Wednesday, we went to Bethlehem: we took Paul, and Sophie to carry him. He slept all the way there and back in the car, but was awake in the church, so he can really say that he saw Jesus's manger. The Church of the Nativity is a beautiful place and very old, built at the time of the Crusades. Of course the Grotto, which is the place where Christ was born, is all decorated, Greek fashion, with hanging lamps and candles, so it is difficult to realise where you are, though I believe it is really the true place: no-one has doubts about it as they have about the site of the Holy Sepulchre. We saw the shop where the mother-of-pearl beads are made, and bought a little cross for Paul.

There is a little cafe at Bethlehem called Good View. When we had tea it was almost like having tea in an English village. We were shown on to a little balcony looking out to the most gorgeous view of hills and terraces and the Dead Sea and the mountains in the distance.

We are looking for a new house, one with a garden for Paul to play in. Everyone moves here in August, so we have begun to look round with the rest.

Cliff is doing well; his pet work at the moment is the Citadel; he is trying to get into the bottom of David's Tower, where there is an immense block which has no opening visible, so he is digging through the floor of the upper roof to try and get in that way. There is great excitement today because they have come upon a crack through which comes a draught, so there must be another opening somewhere.

3rd May

I heard Mrs Philip Snowden lecture at the Ladies Club on her visit to Russia and the Bolsheviks: I enjoyed her very much.

On Tuesday we had a Russian to dinner. He is call Melnicoff and is a sculptor: he did the Allenby bust at Beersheba. He lives in a little room over the Damascus Gate.

15th May

On Sunday, we had two artists to tea, a Mr and Mrs Bomberg. They only arrived on Friday, and Cliff met them because they were looking for rooms in which to put their things. They are quite young and very nice indeed, we hope to see them often. Whilst they were here we had quite an exciting adventure. Cliff has been doing a little housing scheme for the continuation of a Jewish quarter just near here, for a man called Mr Kandinoff. Quite suddenly, on Sunday afternoon, Kandinoff sent a car with a message to Cliff 'would he go and lay the foundation stone'. Cliff said he could not go without his guests, so we all went. It was fun. There were crowds of Russian Jews in wonderful velvet gabardines and astrakhan caps and women in all the colours of the rainbow, it was most gay. Cliff put in a large stone and we all put little ones around it. Then we were all fed on cake and Turkish delight and sticky sweets, and had our photos taken in a large group. A sheep had been killed in the approved fashion for a feast in the evening, and this was laid out in state in front of the group.

24th May

There is great distress across the road: the old man there has only one son who has just had a girl baby; they are very miserable, they have all been waiting for a boy. These people are queer about babies. Cliff's gardener's wife has just had a girl, and the husband told us quite solemnly that he didn't scold her! The Moslems on the other side of us had a boy baby not long ago, and the day it was born there was dancing and singing and all sorts of rejoicings.

On the Moslems' feast of Ramadan they have all been fasting for a whole month between the hours of 3.00am and 6.00pm. At 6.00, they have a huge meal (Mr and Mrs Johnson went to their Moslem neighbours for dinner and they had a whole sheep) and then sing and dance at each others' houses for the rest of the night. The minarets were all lit up and guns were fired when the fast began and ended. On the night when the landlord's wife gave a party, Sophie and I went down to visit her. It was fun. Of course there were no men present. The women all dressed in most awful European clothes; there was a young bride in a wonderful creation of bright pink satin. We all sat round the edge of the room and everyone talked and looked at me, then they began playing the oude (which is rather like a mandolin) and singing and dancing. Arabic music is rather nice when you get used to it. The accompaniment goes on all the time, then someone will begin to sing a verse by herself, then they will all sing together and clap to the music, then someone will get up and dance: it's most amusing. I enjoyed myself thoroughly, it was a pity Cliff could not be there too.

PS   Cliff is studying a map of the world to see where we can go next.

1st June

Tomorrow we celebrate the King's birthday: in the morning we go to St. George's to a 'solemn service' and in the afternoon to a reception in the Municipal Gardens. Mr and Mrs Luke (Assistant Governor and his wife) are host and hostess, as Storrs is still away. His mother is dead. By the way, we hear that Storrs is engaged to a widow with six children!

Cliff is busy at present taking down a horrible eyesore in the city in the shape of a Turkish clock tower, and putting it in a more or less inconspicuous position: he does get some queer jobs.

I must tell you about the exciting time we had yesterday. We went to a fellaheen wedding. Our little milk girl (aged 15) was being married, and her father, who is one of Cliff's gardeners, was very keen that we should go. He wanted us to stay all night, but of course that is impossible with Paul. We set off about 3.30 escorted by Mustapha, the father, we three, Sophie and Cliff's clerk Stern. We rode out into most beautiful country, all bare rolling hills and valleys full of olive and fig trees, to a point where we were to be met by donkeys. However no donkeys arrived, but three horses.

This was most exciting. Sophie (who has ridden anything from a donkey to a camel) went on the first, carrying Paul, Cliff had the friskiest one, and galloped on by himself, and I came along behind, my horse being ignominiously led by a man with a rope; this was perhaps as well as I had never ridden a horse before. We went up and down the most precipitous places and climbed over rocks and stones, and it was all very exciting. I thoroughly enjoyed myself. I discovered afterwards that I was riding the bridegroom's horse. In about half an hour we arrived at the village, a collection of little stone houses with domed roofs and tiny windows, just built in a group on no fixed plan. At the beginning of the village, the women were standing, and as we came up the hill, they sang us a little chant of welcome. We were escorted to a one-roomed house prepared with a few chairs and cushions and a table set with food specially for us. There was white bread, cheese and olives, peaches and sweet biscuits, and beer and soda water to drink. When we arrived, the bridegroom was having a bath (this was an event) and being dressed by his friends, while women stood outside and sang to him. We put Paul to sleep on some cushions, with Sophie on guard, whilst we went to see the fun. Presently, out came the bridegroom, all dressed up in clean clothes and with a blue silk handkerchief round his head and blue lines painted under his eyes. He was set on his horse all decked with flowers, and the procession started. We led the way with Mustapha and an Arab who spoke English: he told us all about the great things he had done in the war against the Turks, and how the French captured a whole village 'all through me'. He had a wonderful imagination. After us came all the men of the village, the bridegroom on a horse, followed by the mother of the bride, who showered him with barley which she carried on a big raffia tray, to keep off the evil eye, in other words to prevent anyone stealing him from her daughter. After this came all the women singing. So we processed all round the village and back again. Afterwards, we saw women dancing, had our feast and then were allowed to see the bride. She is rather indescribable, but looked very fine in her embroidered dress of dark red with silk skirt and sleeves. Her necklaces and bracelets were most barbaric, and her hands and feet dyed red with henna. We shook hands with her and gave her presents, Paul holding two 5 piastre pieces in his little hand. Then unfortunately, it was time to go home, We missed the ceremony and the revelling that followed, and which goes on all through the night.

4th July

Our new house, Beit Musa... Cliff is drawing a plan... The crosses in the front rooms mean that they are vaulted: vaulted rooms are lovely, and are typical of this country. The walls are over a yard thick, so we have fine window sills in all the rooms; in the bedrooms we use them for wash stands and dressing tables... Our garden has no flowers in at present but lots of trees. There is a fir and cypress avenue from the gate to the front door, also we have a vine, an almond tree, a pepper tree an olive tree, a mulberry tree and a fig tree.

12th July

We have been trying to help our washerwoman, Shamsi: she has two big sons, two small sons and a little girl of ten. They all live in one room and feed on bread and cheese and melon: isn't it dreadful? Her eldest daughter is married to a lemonade seller. One of the big sons is out of work – Cliff is going to give him a gardening job – and we have got the little girl here to help Sophie. She is only ten, but she can do an astonishing amount of cleaning and scrubbing, and I am trying to teach her to lay tables, as of course she hasn't the ghost of a notion how to do this: she is probably used to eating off the floor, but she is very bright and learns quickly.

Letters from Elizabeth in Jerusalem and on a trip to Syria

22nd July

It is all perfectly beautiful! Eunice hasn't half described it. In a way, of course, it is indescribable.

We had a beautiful service at St. George's this morning 'making Paul a Christian' as Sophie describes it... Eunice and Paul came in, and we had the baptism proper. It is rather long for a baby but Paul quite enjoyed it. He joined in the singing of the hymn, and when the Bishop expressed the hope that he (Paul) would renounce the world, the flesh and the devil, Paul grunted acquiescence. He was just becoming a little bored and restless when it came time for the Bishop to take him and christen him. This revived his interest. He gazed with wonder at the Bishop while he dabbed him three times with water (God the Father, dab, God the Son, dab, and God the Holy Ghost, dab). After the ceremony the Bishop (B. MacInnes) insisted that we stood at the door so that every one could see the baby. I was holding the fat lump and got very tired of it. How much he was admired! His bright smile and intelligent expression and fat arms and legs. The Bishop was charmed with him, and Paul was equally charmed with the Bishop's shining crozier. The Bishop dashed off for his camera and insisted on photographing Paul, then and there, holding the crozier. Then we all adjourned for tea at the Archdeacon's, such a crowd of gay gentlemen and ladies, including Colonel Storrs and his wife, Lady Clayton, wife of the Chief Secretary, and Paul who was handed round until he was tired. Then we took him home, right in the noon day heat. This house is beautifully cool, however. The stone walls are a yard thick and the rooms very large and lofty, with vaulted ceilings.

1st August

It is the feast of Elijah today, whether of his being fed by ravens or his ascent to Heaven I cannot tell. The Moslems are not really concerned in this, but they join in all feasts. Sophie (Christian) has had the day off. Such gay doings, families in groups picnicking under every olive tree, with their donkey with its gay tasselled saddle tied to a low bough, and slung from another bough, a tiny hammock with the baby in it, and a cloth laid for the bread and olives they had brought. No doubt they would supplement this fare by purchases from the various stalls that had sprung up along the road: lemonade, rissoles, sweetmeats, a savoury mince, fried to order on an open grill… across the road the bare tawdry church… We pushed our way through the throng of people, no-one in the least interested in us though we were the only Europeans about. We met Harrison's Arab servant Jacob, who toured with us for a while (*Austen Harrison was a well-known architect*). After about an hour of it, we found another gharry and drove home. Paul is quite a seasoned traveller. It does not disturb his night's rest nor his equable temper.

We are planning a holiday into Syria, Beirut, Damascus and Baalbec. Eunice contemplates quite calmly the packing of the baby paraphernalia: pram, cot, bath, swan, et cetera.

We are late tonight because Shereef Effendi stayed until after eleven. He is the Headmaster of the big boys' school here for Moslems and Christians (not Jews). He is Mohammedan. We asked him why the Moslems have charge of the

Holy Sepulchre. It seems that the Turks were puzzled as to whether to make Latin or Greek or Abyssinian or Coptic churches the keepers, knowing that jealousy and possible feuds would arise, so they gave the charge to a neutral religious body. The British continued the custom. So at the entrance of the Holy Sepulchre Church there is a porch lined with cushions, where the Moslem guards sleep.

We visited the Tombs of the Kings and Solomon's Quarries, both most interesting. On our way there, we met Mr and Mrs Storrs on horseback with an escort of three outriders. All five stopped to speak to us. The Governor hailed Eunice with 'Well, how is the Apostle?' We are going to tea with them today. The Tombs of the Kings are supposed to be the tombs of the Kings of Judah, but are probably the tombs of Queen Helena of Adiabene and her son Isates and his 24 sons. She was converted to Judaism. They are hewn out of solid rock. At the inner entrance is a real rolling stone in it's socket. We took candles into the catacombs: they are empty, just showing the shelves where the sarcophagi were. One sarcophagus was found there and is now in the Louvre.

The quarries were, if anything, the more exciting and terrifying. They go for a long way under the city, and are just like the limestone caves of the Ingleton district, Yorkshire. We entered by the Damascus Gate and took candles. The limestone rock is quite soft where it is dark and wet, but hardens on coming out into the air. Some people suppose the quarries go right to the Temple area a mile away. It was from these quarries that the stone was cut for Solomon's Temple. You can see the places where the great stones have been quarried and little holes in the rock where lamps are suppose to have stood.

9th August
Trip to Syria – Haifa

Haifa is more continental than oriental. It is more a Mediterranean seaside resort than an Eastern city. It is a strange mixture, showing the influence of Arab, Jew, German, French, Italian and now English. We walked through the oriental part yesterday afternoon, but it is squalid without being picturesque and there is such a jumble of types of shop in the suq. One shop was a small dark room, and opposite the door was a hole through which we could see a furnace burning... a great oven. On the floor were two heaps of round cakes, one of unbaked cakes laid in rows between layers of dirty sacking, the other of baked ones, very puffy and lovely light brown. One of the boys was wiping them over with a dirty rag which he dipped in a saucer of liquid which made the cake shine. They looked very light and good.

We walked down to the sea just before dinner, and thought Paul looked surprised to see such a big bath. This morning we got up at six and went down to the sea in bathing costumes... when Eunice and Cliff were in the water, I undressed Paul and gave him to them… he didn't mind at all, but he likes the wash basin better.

12th August
Alieh

We are in the strangest place now, but perhaps it would seem less strange to you than would some of the other places we have stayed in. Here the orient had never established itself, but France has. And this is the Monte Carlo of Syria. We were not told this when we were told of this beautiful place in the Lebanon. But I shall not readily forget it, for my bedroom windows are just about ten metres from one of the Casinos… and they gamble all night. Cliff remarked that the French have impressed themselves far more on Syria than have the English on Palestine, but I understand from a fellow guest here that the French were in Alieh and Beirut before the war and that the Syrians have always liked the French.

The drive from Haifa to Beirut was an experience. The road from Haifa to Acre is marked on the map with a thick yellow line, but there is no road at all. We ran along the shore and, more often than not, actually in the sea.

Arrived at Baalbec and had tea; perfectly lovely; splendid hotel; beautiful scenery; Roman ruins; we shall stay as long as possible.

August
Damascus

We are all in mourning tonight because we have lost the dear old swan. Paul doesn't realise his loss yet. We think it was nipped off the perambulator this afternoon while we were petting a tiny baby donkey. Paul has certainly learnt this week what fun it is to drop things over the carriage side. I don't know what he will find to bite now. Well it has had a short life and a gay one.

16th August

Who was it who spoke of the rivers of Damascus! The first sign of Damascus for us was a greenness and a river. We had motored from Baalbec through astonishing, barren country, at first along the plain between Lebanon and anti-Lebanon, then striking to the left over anti-Lebanon we climbed through bare red hills by a narrow winding pass… then came to higher hills of rugged limestones: such desolation (rather like the Buttertubs but wilder). Once we passed a fountain that had been built for thirsty travellers and it was crowded with black goats, all pushing and scrambling and standing on their hind legs for a drink.

17th August

We think we shall stay here four days and then go home by train via Haifa. We shall pass the Sea of Galilee at Samakh and cross the Jordan. I wonder what impression this is all having on little Paul?... He was so very happy jogging through the Damascus suq. If anything, the noise and smells and colours were more exciting than in Jerusalem. He waved his arms and legs about and crowed and smiled. We had such a procession following us. Some boys followed every bit of the way, and we walked miles. The 'street that is called straight' must be over a mile. It is lined with bazaars of all kinds, smiths making iron tools and wrought iron gateways, men at the simplest lathes carving the wood part of the narguiles, others weaving coloured belts for camels and donkeys. Workers in beaten brass and inlay, others making real leather shoes. We came out of the city at Bab Sharki and walked for a while outside the city. This was a false turn on our part. We found ourselves toiling in 'dark white' dust, six inches deep and, to make matters worse, a donkey was having an especially luxurious dust bath in it, legs in air. At the earliest possible moment we turned again into the city and, tired and dusty, all tumbled into a gharry and were driven back to the hotel.

21st August

Here we are home again safe and sound. We came to Haifa from Damascus by train on Monday, 7.00am - 6.00pm. We spent the night at Gassman's Hotel... left Haifa at 10.30am and came by the rockiest route through fields of thistle and rocky river beds (we were nearly bounced to pulp) as far as Jenin: after that there is a good road.

We have travelled wonderfully easily; people have been kind and hotels comfortable. Paul has been welcomed with open arms everywhere. The old Turk who was our host at Baalbec used to open his arms and say 'Come along, you Governor of Transjordania – you will be a Governor one day I am sure, you have the head!'

Cliff's Citadel is most interesting, one feels there may be anything beneath all that debris. He has cleared a lot away. He is going to explore the cisterns for underground passages. Everyone believes there is buried treasure there.

You would have a fit if you saw Paul careering through the old city in his perambulator up and down steps, rollicking over cobbles and great stones, among such a jumble of men, women and children and donkeys and goats and sheep, such colours and sound and smells (stinks). The Arabs turn round and smile at him – they seem to like babies – the veiled women stroke his hands: one lifted her veil and kissed him suddenly. (As Eunice says, it is all right if she can see the face first.)

We called on Mohammed Jepshi, their old landlord, last Friday. Paul went in his kafieh, which the landlord gave him for a birthday present. We went into the bedroom across the courtyard to see the lady of the house. Eunice congratulated her on her new bed. Usually the Arab's wife sleeps on the floor by his bed but Mohammed is very humane and advanced, and had bought her a bed just like his own.

We had a nice picnic at Solomon's Pools on Friday. While Eunice and Paul made tea, Cliff and I collected plants. The country was like Derbyshire for the limestone terraces. We passed Rachel's Tomb and skirted Bethlehem. The fauna and flora of the pools is extraordinarily like that of the ditches on the sandhills, even to frogs and horse leeches and water boatmen: isn't it odd? I came home and read Ecclesiastes. It is interesting to read the Bible in Jerusalem. Eunice is always reading it at odd moments, and I've got into the habit too.

Letters from Eunice

31st August
We saw Elizabeth off safely at 8.15 on Wednesday morning. She was hoping to sail on the 30th. How these six weeks have flown, I can't believe she has been and gone again.

9th September
An Architectural Society is going to be started in Jerusalem, and we have had two meetings to discuss it and draw up its charter: the second meeting was at our house on Thursday night. So far there are only seven members, Kauffman, Miss Cohen, Cliff and I, a Russian architect whose name I couldn't possibly remember except that it ends with a 'wski' and two others, Kornburg and Salant. They are all very enthusiastic, and jabber away in German, waving their arms about and gesticulating in true foreign fashion, except the Russian, who sits very solemnly and quietly and solidly smokes cigarettes, one after the other, till you would think he'd be smoked inside.

13th September
Cliff is very busy at present preparing a Civic Survey. It is an immense work, and includes every scrap of information about Jerusalem. He will have to do it all himself, as there is no-one who could help... Paul was seven months old yesterday, doesn't time more than fly?

6th October
Cliff has kept the pictures of Tutankhamen's tomb. Perhaps we shall find a second Tut in Jerusalem. Cliff is hoping to find a sarcophagus, with Herod inside, in the Citadel. Prof. Macalister is here, ready to start work. He is very interested in the Citadel, and says if Cliff will supervise the work and arrange for labour, he will do some excavating there. It would be fun; they will, perhaps, get into that closed room, where there was a draught, do you remember?

The Jews have just been having their Feast of Tabernacles. They all built little tents outside their houses and decorated them with our Christmas decorations and flowers and leaves et cetera and live there for a fortnight; it is supposed to be very unlucky if it does not rain during the fortnight and the Jews all over the world are praying for rain. It did rain, but only a very little.

I forgot in my last letter to tell you about our day in Ramallah. We went by car at nine in the morning, a lovely little ride, and were met by our host, who took us to his house, to a room on the roof, with windows on every side, the most gorgeous view all round, and we could see the sea! It was delightfully cool and we sat on a little balcony all morning. We watched a funeral procession that passed beneath the balcony, all men, led by priests. The women stood a little way off doing the most weird dance in a huge circle, clapping their hands and chanting the virtues of the dead man. It really looked rather festive, and very like the dance we saw at Jameely's wedding. We had an exciting lunch, all men except me: our host, Cliff, an awful rogue of an Arab who told us funny stories, and the Mexican Consul, a most enormous fat man, who ate and ate and ate… We were waited on by the host's father, who used to be cook to an Englishman, a most picturesque old thing with striped frock and orange turban and long white beard. We began lunch with a kind of hors d'oeuvres of olives and quail and tomatoes: we ate the quail with a large fork and fingers. Then we had a succession of different dishes: chicken, potatoes, stuffed marrows, stuffed cucumbers, cutlets, beans, all handed round one after the other, with no respect for courses, until our plates were overladen. We finished with grapes and coffee, and then the old man apologised for not giving us a very good meal because he had to attend the funeral! In the afternoon I dressed up in Ramallah native dress: the most beautiful embroidery was worked by one of the household. But the head-dress is appalling, trimmed with about 200 silver and gold coins. It is dreadfully heavy: I understand now why these women walk and stand so straight, they can't do otherwise.

6th October
I can hardly believe that Paul will be eight months old next week. I wish you could see him now, he is getting nicer and nicer. His top teeth look very near – they will come first – this is unlucky, according to the Arabs, and Sophie says I must give him something old, belonging to a grandmother or grandfather, if his top ones grow first. These people are absolutely steeped in superstition. They say my next baby will be a boy because Paul has a double crown.

20th October
I must tell you what happened on Thursday. Cliff and I were in a little shop in the suq looking for stuff for Paul's coat. Just as we were going out, the boy in the

Eunice with Paul

Cliff with Paul

shop, who spoke fairly good English, said to Cliff, 'Please Sir, how long is it from Manchester to Leeds?' We were so surprised. Cliff told him about one and a half hours, and he said very doubtfully 'No, six hours I think.' In the end he was convinced that it was a very quick train, and then he asked how far to Manchester from 'Piccadilly'. His next question was 'There is plenty of material in Leeds?' I asked if he was going, and he said yes.

Cliff is busy drawing a plan of Allenby Square. I told you he had been to a camp at Ludd. He had quite a good time, and met there the Mr Herford, Alan

Taylor's friend, that Mother once asked about. There are plenty of architects in Palestine. Prof. Garstang has brought one out to do drawings for him, a Mr Horsfield.

6th November
Antiquities have had two exciting discoveries. One is a most beautiful Greek sarcophagus, unfinished but beautifully carved on two sides with figures – a battle scene – very valuable and the best thing ever found in Palestine. The other discovery is a Jewish tomb, found by some workmen, quite by accident, just outside Jerusalem. The tomb contains 19 ossari (little stone coffins containing the bones of the departed) dated from the first century BC. My birthday on Thursday, 24 years, isn't it old?

11th December
Cliff is having a time, at present, putting up the Turkish Tower in Post Office Square. He has got out a scheme, and began work yesterday.

12th December
I left Paul for Sophie to feed for the first time today. We went down to Gethsemene to meet the Governor and an architect, and see a new church that is being built for the Latins, a hideous thing, very big and pretentious and rather a desecration, I think. We went in Storrs' car back to his house, as he was entertaining all the architects in Jerusalem to tea to discuss the new association. There was only one other woman architect there, Miss Cohen. Mrs Storrs was acting as hostess of course. On Saturday we are going to Government House to tea: I am afraid we shall be bored.

19th December
The rain has arrived, rain and wind for three days, an absolute hurricane all the time: remember we live on top of a mountain. It was needed. Water was being bought into Jerusalem from Nablus and sold at a piastre a tin. We have been fairly fortunate getting water from the top of the road, our ration being six tins a day.

28th December
I want to tell you all about our Christmas. At eight o'clock, we set off for Bethlehem. It was a glorious night, cloudless and a big moon. The car took us nearly to the church, then we walked through a little courtyard where St. George's choir and others were singing carols. We were given candles and books and joined in the singing, and after this we went into one of the chapels and sang 'Christians Awake', We came into the church itself just as the service was beginning: the place was packed, but we found a Bethlehemite who knows us,

and he guided us to special seats at the front so we saw everything splendidly. I can't describe the service. Have you been to catholic mass? Prayers and chants, 'the bell and the book' and amens and paternosters. The chief figure was a cardinal elect, a most imposing figure, very good-looking and wearing the most gorgeous robes and a red cardinal's hat. The singing and chanting went on until about 11.30, and we all got thoroughly sleepy and bored, when things began to happen, so we woke up again. All sorts of garments were taken from the altar, and each garment given to a little boy in a surplice, then six little boys carrying cloak, stole, hat, sceptre et cetera, marched to the Cardinal, and he was undressed and dressed again in new robes, and there were lots more prayers and taking off of hats and putting them on again and walking round, and then at midnight a little bell rang, a little curtain was drawn over the altar and there was a little baby. Jesus was born. That was the climax. We went home: I believe afterwards there is a procession of priests to the Grotto but we did not wait for that. We got home at two in the morning: Cliff and I drank cocoa and gave each other our Christmas presents.

5

1924

This year begins and ends with problematic questions relating to decisions about staying in Palestine, on the one hand, and staying in England for the birth of the second child on the other. In January, Eunice writes, 'Talking of coming home, I had better break the news at once: we shall probably come back here for another two years. I do hope Mother and Father won't be very upset.' Later, in England, she wishes that she was back in Jerusalem.

Clearly there were expectations by her parents that a two-year stay in Palestine would be all. But Eunice and Cliff enjoyed the life, and Cliff's work was beginning to show the possibilities of commissions for buildings in private practice. The experience in England at the end of the year must have hardened their resolve to stay in Jerusalem, for no further reference is made to going home when the new two-year contract was up.

The move to a third house, Beit Syriac in the Street of the Prophets, a little to the west of the old city, must have helped feelings for the future. The house was a very pleasant one, near the old city and large enough eventually to hold Cliff's office, and with a garden. They were to stay there for six years before moving to a house near Bethlehem.

This was also a fairly quiet time politically and, in spite of a rise in Jewish immigration, there were no disturbances. But there was always some Arab lawlessness in the hills, and brigands were not uncommon on the roads between the towns. In her descriptions of a trip to Jericho, Eunice does not mention such things, but I remember seeing the remains of low walls that had been built across the road to stop cars, and so rob passengers. No doubt she did not want to alarm her parents.

The journey from Jerusalem to Jericho was one of 37 kilometres, much of it on steeply winding roads, and dropping from 750 metres to 258 metres below sea level, the lowest town on earth, and with a climate far hotter than Jerusalem. On the way down, the Wadi Kelt is a spectacular ravine 150 metres deep, where we used to picnic. The existing town of Jericho was little more than a large village at that time, and a mile away from the old city, which had been an important and fertile place from ancient times until the departure of the Crusaders in 1187.

The Holy Fire, which Eunice describes in her letter of the 2nd of May, was, in the words of Sir Ronald Storrs in his autobiography *Orientations*[3], 'a brilliant mystery, half political, half pagan, marred sometimes by drunkenness, savagery and murder'. It took place on Easter Eve and, during Turkish rule, up to six hundred troops had been used to keep order. It caused great concern to Governor Storrs, not only in the keeping of the peace, but in the religious and political choice of a patriarch who would be acceptable to the many interests who were present. Storrs himself escorted the Archbishop of Mount Sinai on the first British occasion in 1918 and, in his words, 'the few (but fairly hard) blows aimed by the Armenians at the Archbishop were intercepted by my own outstretched arm'.

Eunice returned to England in the autumn, and letters to her mother and sister Elizabeth make clear that she is unhappy. Cliff had to stay behind in Jerusalem to complete work on the clock tower, and was uncertain as to whether he would be able to get home, although in the event he did. I get the sense that this was something of a turning point in career and family life, and that they now saw Jerusalem as having a more permanent place in their lives.

8th January
I suppose you have heard about Sir Ronald Storrs? He was to have taken us to Jericho today with Mr and Mrs Bomberg, but it rained so we could not go… Sophie had been away for the weekend: it was the Greek Christmas, and she went to spend it with her fiance. She is going to be married at the end of the month, so I am looking for another maid. I had hoped that she would stay until we came home, but her fiance, who is a dragoman, hopes to make some money when the tourists come, and they are going to be married on the strength of it.

15th January
Talking of coming home, I had better break the news at once: we shall probably come back here for another two years. I do hope Mother and Father won't be very upset. You see Cliff is just getting into the swing of things. He has got several jobs going: Post Office Square; a few town planning schemes; a possible Roman Catholic church on Mount Zion; and not to mention Jerusalem itself – the survey which is just getting on its feet – so that it seems a tremendous pity to chuck it all and come back to a measly office or something equally uninspiring. Of course, if we were not perfectly happy here, we should not hesitate a minute, but we are, and the place is ripping. I have no objection at all to staying in the Holy City a little longer.

Cliff went to Ramleh near Ludd last Saturday, and had the most exciting time. He went there with the Governor, Harrison and a few others. They were invited to lunch at the Mayor's house, where they had a great feed, the chief dainty being a sheep roasted whole. One of the guests had been known to eat a whole sheep himself. He was a renowned character in the village!

We had a football match here on Wednesday between Palestine and a team from Vienna. Kauffman asked Cliff to go with him and explain the game, as he didn't know anything about it. Cliff said it was awfully difficult, as he didn't think Kauffman had ever played a game of anything in his life.

20th January

On Saturday, we went to Hebron. Cliff had to go with the Governor, so I went too. The car was packed, there were seven of us not counting the chauffeur. Hebron is a lovely old place: it is where Abraham pitched his tent under the oak trees. 'Abraham's oak' is still standing. We had not enough time to see the town itself, but went up to the glass works, which is rather an imposing name for the place, for there is just one little room. It is low and dark, and the six men sit round the little furnace making vases, bracelets, rings et cetera. It is very picturesque, and the glass is lovely. The little vase I sent Elsie for Christmas, and the camel's eye beads we sent her last year were all made at Hebron. The glass is going to be shown in the Palestine Pavilion at the British Empire Exhibition.

We went for a long walk yesterday, dragging Paul up and down the most steep precipitous places. We went down to Gethsemene, past Macalister's excavations and Siloam, and up to Mont Zion. We had tea with Mr Harrison and heard the gramophone... I am just waiting for Mrs Bomberg, who wants some maidenhair (fern?). Soon Paul will be a year old. If anyone wants to send him birthday presents will they please send socks, shoes or sandals?

28th January

We had a wonderful day yesterday. An Armenian, whom Cliff helped, took us and Mr Shiber (an Arab architect) to Jericho and the Jordan. We had a lovely time: all the way there, we were wishing that Elsie was with us, and deciding that she must come to Palestine again, if only to take this trip. The formation of the rocks is most extraordinary: they are folded and curved in the queerest fashion, as if they had been through hundreds of volcanoes and earthquakes. We passed a lot of interesting places on the way: first Bethany, a dear little village on a hillside, very small and peaceful, then the Inn of the Good Samaritan, or Jericho halfway house, and further on the Wadi Kelt. The Wadi Kelt is the most wonderful river valley, the steepest I have ever seen; the sides are precipitous, and very high. At the bottom, the rock is riddled with the caves of hermits who used to live here. It was here that Elijah lived, and I suppose John the Baptist; I don't know what they could have lived on, the land is absolutely barren, a perfect wilderness.

The first view of the Jordan plain is a fine sight, and looks curiously like it does in our picture of Moses. Jericho lies at one side at the foot of the hills, and is just like an oasis, with its oranges, banana groves and big trees. We went straight through Jericho to Allenby Bridge, the only traffic bridge across the Jordan into Transjordania. The country round the river is made of queer sorts of sandhills of dry mud, all cut up by the wind into strange shapes. Nothing grows on it at all, but on each bank of the Jordan there is a line of trees which were all in autumn tints when we were there. We had lunch on the banks of the river. We took Paul's lunch in a thermos. It was beautifully warm: we had started with jerseys and coats, but were able to take them all off again. After lunch, we went back to Jericho. There is a long lane that runs through the town, almost like an English country lane. At one end is present Jericho, and at the other is a big mound which was ancient Jericho. We went into the most lovely garden, all oranges and banana groves with a little stream running through.

After we had seen Jericho we set off for the Dead Sea. On the way, we saw the part of the Jordan where Christ was baptised. I got some Jordan water in a bottle, so if you want anyone to be christened in holy water, I can send you some. When we had been on the way for about ten minutes, we came upon an enormous puddle; the road was flooded, and so we could not get any further. Wasn't it a pity? Still, we had got far enough to see salt lying on the ground like frost. The Mount of Temptation is just above Jericho, and there is a monastery half way up on a ledge of rock which we want to visit one day. Altogether we had a lovely day, but unfortunately it ended with a dreadful catastrophe, we lost the camera. We were heartbroken, and Cliff nearly wept. There will be no more pictures of Paul now, at least not till we get home.

15th February

We are in a state of chaos at the moment. Government House is moving down to the Government building, and this house is wanted for a Government House official, so we have to move out. Don't we change around? I feel rather pleased on the whole, as I want to get a small house that I can more or less run myself. Now that Paul doesn't need so much attention, I shall rather enjoy doing housework again. I quite look forward to the cooking part, inventing dishes like I did at Mossley Hill. Sophie is going on Monday, and I am not getting a new maid until we finally decide what we are going to do. These changes are very exhilarating, we don't stagnate! The only place I don't want to live in is the German Colony, where all the English people live. I have the idea of spending time paying calls and receiving callers, and going to select, but dull, dinner parties.

The Bombergs have a little Bohemia all of their own in two rooms in the old city, and a gorgeous high roof overlooking the whole of Jerusalem. I go to have may picture done, and to drink coffee out of little bowls and eat brown bread and butter made of sheep's milk.

My picture is now finished and I like it. Cliff has only seen it once, but I think he is going to like it too. I don't know whether we shall buy it.

Jerusalem is full of tourists, cars full of people dashing about. They are a funny crowd, American women in furs and frills, all dressed up to the eyes, and most of them so discontented-looking. Some time soon, three hundred English Catholics are coming.

17th February

Yes, Cliff had to be reappointed. His contract has been renewed for another two years. We don't know how long it will be before we come home, but when we do, it is for three months so, allowing for the journeys, we ought to be quite two months at home.

27th February

We had a Bohemian lunch at the Bombergs, Paul included. They are funny people, absolutely on their last crust, literally living on tea and toast, when the Governor finally decided (he had been considering for weeks) to buy their big picture for £100. So they were up in the air when we went, and we had a big feast. Paul quite entered into the spirit of the meal, and sat in an upturned coffee stool. He had a finger biscuit in one hand and a cutlet bone in the other, having a bite of each in turn, and looking the picture of perfect – but sticky – bliss.

The Bombergs, being millionaires for the time being, are off to Jericho to paint more pictures. We hope to go and visit them some time. The Armenian who took us before felt rather responsible for the loss of Cliff's camera, and has presented him with a new one, but it is not a very good one. Still, we shall get some snaps of Paul.

I am sorry to say that we cannot come home until August after all. The Governor is going home in June for two months, and Cliff cannot have leave until he comes back. I'm sorry to disappoint you, but it can't be helped: Governors can do these things.

We had a most exciting time on Tuesday. We found a hurt jackal in the little shed in the garden. Such a queer looking creature, with great yellow eyes and a huge mouth. We sent for Said (owner of the corner shop) to come and kill him because he was hurt and did not seem able to move. Said came in great excitement with two other men, and they stood around the door and began poking him with a stick. I don't know what good they thought that would do. What happened was that the creature suddenly sprang up and ran away, then there was a hullabaloo! Abdul and Yousef, (Johnson's servants) came out and they all started dashing about looking for it, for it seems that Arabs eat jackals. Anyway, it was hopeless, they could not find it, and so gave up. That night we had a pack of about five or six crying near the house, it sounded horribly uncanny, just like babies crying. I wonder if they came to look for the hurt one, or if they were hunting it out of the pack because it was sick? Next day the poor thing was in the shed again, so Cliff went and borrowed a revolver and shot it. We could not get anyone to move it just then, so it stayed in the shed all day, and what excitement that caused. We had quite a stream of people coming to see it. I can't see anything very thrilling about a dead jackal, but we had visits from small boys, from men, and even Moslem women.

One day we went to Bethlehem to visit some native people who have a big house there. They were interesting people, who had been to America and had many relatives there. They were extremely rich, and fetched and brought us home in a lovely car which they had got in America. One of our hosts was a young man who had not been to Bethlehem since he was twelve; he came back three months ago to be married and was most unhappy. Bethlehem, he found, was rather too much of a change from New York, so he was going back as soon as he possibly could, and taking his wife with him. We were only paying them an afternoon call, so to speak, and so we got rather a shock when at about 4.30 they announced that lunch was ready, and presented us with a six course meal!

March

We have got a lovely new house, Beit Syriac, in the Street of the Prophets. Just by wonderful luck we have a house that we have looked at with longing ever since coming to Jerusalem. It belongs to (or rather its tenant was) the Bishop's sister, Miss MacInnes, and she is going back home to live. It is an old house, more romantic-looking than our present one, with four rooms upstairs and a kitchen et cetera downstairs. The staircase is outside in a most delightful little courtyard: this is paved, and has one flower bed running along the side, with a rambler rose and a vine. There is a flat roof over one room, and we can see the Mountains of

The Street of the Prophets

The Street of the Prophets

Beit Syriac

Beit Syriac

Moab. In fact it is a lovely little house and we are very glad to be going into it. It has a better position too, nearer the town, and is just opposite the Governor's house. We cannot go in until June.

24th March

Last week Cliff, Paul and I went on a lovely picnic into the hills on the way to Bethlehem. Everything is green now, and Paul sat on the grass. We sat him in the middle of the red anemones and he loved it. They are so beautiful, and such a bright bright red: of course he picks them and pulls off all their petals, but that does not matter. We met such a queer man on the way. I think that he must have been a second day adventist or a religious maniac, probably the latter. He said he was trying to bring on a second Reformation in England, and that his chief aim in life was to bring about the downfall of the Catholics and the Greeks... he said there was going to be a great war in 1927... and that Christ was coming again in 1932. In fact, if Paul had not yelled with impatience, I think we should have been listening still.

1st April

We hunted for a home for the next two or three months, and found a house in the German Colony. It belongs to people called Baker who are going on leave for three months. The next problem was where to stay from 28th March until 8th of April, so we decided on the German Hospice, which is just next door to the house, and here we are. Mother, you would love to be here. The German Hospice is really the Convent of St. Charles, and of course everyone belonging to it is a nun, that is except a funny little man called Stanislau, a sort of door keeper, and an old grey-bearded gardener. The nuns seem to do everything themselves: cooking, washing and cleaning. The place is spotlessly clean and the garden perfectly wonderful. The German Colony, where most of the English people live, is not like real Jerusalem, it has little German red-roofed houses, and each house has a garden. There are heaps of trees and flowers, so that the roads are quite shady. It is a very nice place, and a change, though we both say we wouldn't like to live here permanently, because it isn't enough like Jerusalem.

Cliff had a town planning meeting today (April 1st) so he took a large drawing of the most crazy looking building for a cinema on the Mount of Olives, and presented it for the Governor's signature! The Governor appreciated being made an April fool, and sent it up to Sir Gilbert Clayton. What he thought of it, they will know tomorrow.

23rd April

Today is the Greek Good Friday, and this afternoon we went to the Sepulchre. The celebrations of the Latins are tame compared with those of the Greeks. When we arrived, the church was packed with all sorts of people. There was a procession, rather a mixed one, but with plenty of incense and velvet robes et cetera. As they held a very short service at each traditional spot, I think they must have been following the story of the crucifixion. We were there about 5.30, and found them just going to the Calvary, which is, as you know, in the big church. Afterwards, they made their way to the place of the anointing and so to the Sepulchre. We had not time to stay very long, but just heard a little of the service: the singing was execrable. The small boys – and the men – seemed to be just trying to make as much noise as they possibly could, regardless of time and tune. It is all hopelessly un-Christian, but intensely interesting. The queer old priests in their velvet and gold; the hundreds of golden lamps with lights of red, blue and green; the crowds pushing all around and the great old grey church for a background makes a most exciting picture. Paul loved it all. What things this baby is seeing. I wonder what effect it will have on him. He wasn't the only baby by any means: Arabic babies were all over the place, running about or sitting on the floor.

2nd May

I must tell you all about the Holy Fire, but how to begin I don't know. It was absolutely the most wonderful thing that I have ever seen, and there I feel I should stop, but I must try and give you a little idea of the affair nevertheless. To begin with, you must know that the main part of the Holy Sepulchre Church, where the ceremony takes place, is circular, with a dome and very high galleries all around, the highest one being in the dome itself, and here were we. The Sepulchre is inside a little gold chamber in the middle of the circular building, and on each of two sides is a little round hole, like a porthole. Through here the fire comes. Our party consisted of Mrs Garstang, Mrs Gem-Smith, Miss Dixon (Prof.'s secretary), Miss Marsden (Meroe's governess), Meroe and myself (Cliff staying at home to look after Paul)... armed with camp stools and a good supply of choc. We met at 9.30, and proceeded to walk over the roofs of Jerusalem until we got to the church, where we waited for ages in a great crowd. Then after much pushing and scrambling and running about, and getting into the wrong dome and getting out again, and bullying our perfectly helpless guide, we got to our right places. We could look down on to everyone's heads and see everything. The church was packed, so that it was just one mass of heads. You can imagine what excitement there was, everyone talking and shouting and sometimes starting a little song and dance. And in one corner, near the Sepulchre, was a picnic! Mothers and babies having lunch who had been there all night. Miss Dixon was just remarking how quiet it was this year, when suddenly there was a huge commotion. About twenty or thirty men were pushing their way into the crowd, bringing the runners. The runners are men who carry the fire all over the country, especially to Bethlehem. Before the war, the light was taken all the way to Russia, and I think it is still taken to Greece. The Bethlehem runners literally run all the way to Bethlehem with lighted candles. They have men round them to keep off evil-minded people who try to blow out their candles. Three runners stand by the Sepulchre with their arms (and candles) right inside the hole (so it really seems quite easy for the Patriarch to light them with a box of matches doesn't it?)

Soon the soldiers came along to make room for the procession. It didn't seem possible, but they did it by persistent pushing: I think the people must have either melted into the wall or gone several degrees thinner to make room. The procession began with about four men clearing the way; then followed six British officers, three abreast and walking casually along arm-in-arm as if they were going for an afternoon stroll. Next came twelve boys carrying large banners with pictures of the crucifixion, followed by some priests in black, and twelve in most wonderful gold and silver brocade robes, these latter ones were a bodyguard for the Patriarch. The Patriarch is lovely, a good-looking old man with a long white beard. He was dressed in shining white satin, and on his head he had a gold crown set with four big green stones. More priests and banners followed.

This procession walked round three times. At the third time round, the passage closed up automatically and immediately. With great pushing and scuffling a small passage was made for the runners, and then the excitement began. At the door of the Sepulchre, the Patriarch stops and takes off his crown and robes and is examined (rather superficially) by the Governor, to see that he has no unspiritual lights about his person. He then goes to the Sepulchre, and the door is shut. By this time, the excitement is simply intense, everyone is strung up to the highest pitch and just ready to burst, the suspense is terrible! Quite suddenly all the bells begin to ring, great clangs one after another, and almost immediately a runner rushes out waving a lighted candle, then another comes, and more and more and more. Everyone began to clap and shout and dance and sing, and all the candles were alight and the church ablaze. Whole bundles of candles were dropped by strings from the balconies so the lights were up to the very top. Then the excitement died down; the people ran out with their candles and the church became full of smoke when it was left to the less important processions of Armenians and Copts.

9th May

Cliff had to go to Bethlehem on Tuesday to see a man about a shop and house he is building there. The man is one of those Bethlehemites who spend a lot of time in America. He came to Cliff in a car, and so Paul and I went too, to his house, and saw some queer people. A very religiously-inclined gentleman in a frock coat and check trousers, who lived in Peru and only spoke Arabic and Spanish and a fat mother with a very squeally baby whom she treated abominably. When it yelled, she jogged it vigorously up and down and then stuffed sticky Turkish delight into its mouth. They were all very pleased to see us, and sorry when we would not stay. Yesterday, the man rolled up to the Governorate and presented Cliff with a gold watch and chain which, of course, Cliff promptly refused. However, in the afternoon, a mysterious package was left addressed to 'Dear Babe Paul' and inside was the gold watch.

We loved Nazareth: Elsie will remember the journey there. It was greener than when we went before. We saw heaps of storks, fields full of them… Nazareth seems all churches and convents. We visited the shrines on the Place of the Annunciation and a room where Jesus is supposed to have preached. There wasn't much time, as it is a four-hour drive.

20th May

We shall see our new house this afternoon, as we are going to an 'at home' at Miss MacInnes. She is going the second week in June, so we shall get in about the beginning of July. Everyone envies our new house: it really is the most romantic place.

23rd May

The Governor is getting a wireless set, so perhaps we shall be able to listen in before we come home after all. We shouldn't hear English though, as it comes from Rome and Cairo.

The Bombergs came to dinner Saturday. They have had a most exciting time. The Governor sent them to Petra to paint, and they were provided with an escort which they appear to have been more frightened of than the Bedouins themselves. They are going back again in about a week, and intend to stay about six months. It is an exciting journey: horseback all the way and nights spent in the black tents. We are longing to go to Petra, but we can't because of Paul. We are going to leave him for the day on Saturday to go to Ain Farah. It is a little village with lots of water where we can bathe. We go by donkey, a two-hour ride. On Sunday we went to Ain Kareem, a little village with lots of trees and gardens. It is the prettiest little place built all up the side of a hill. Nearby the village is the supposed birthplace of John the Baptist.

6th June

We take over our new house tomorrow. It is going to be whitewashed, and we shall paint it ourselves. We are going to have a picnic there and a good look round.

The Governor went on leave on Wednesday, and has invited Paul and me to go and play in his garden whenever we like. The garden is a lovely place, and just across the road from the new house. We went to the Governor's tea party on the

King's birthday. There were 700 people invited! Everyone was there, tea in the garden and the police band playing. In the intervals, the band from Transjordania marched around playing bagpipes. It was very gay, as a lot of the men were in uniform and all the officers of the fleet were there. The fleet is at Jaffa, and the sailors came by train on Monday. Paul and I went to the station to see them arrive. Cliff has been dreadfully busy these last few weeks. He goes off at 7.30 in the morning (we get up at 6.00) and often doesn't come home till five, sometimes later.

24th June

We went to Hebron on Sunday afternoon with our Bethlehem-American friend Mr Hendel and his wife. He got permission, through Arab friends, to go into the mosque there. This a very special privilege, as it is very difficult for Europeans to be allowed in. The mosque is most interesting, surrounded by a very big wall which the Jews believe to have been built by Solomon. The Jews come and wail there every Friday night, just as they do in Jerusalem. They are only allowed to come up to the fifth step, and they wail at a particularly large stone (8 metres long). The mosque is supposed to have been built over the cave of Machpelah, where Sarah and Abraham and Isaac and Jacob were buried. There is certainly a cave underneath which can be seen through a hole in the floor of the mosque. The bones were found here by Empress Helena, and none can enter the cave now except the Moslems, who have built huge shrines over the place where the tombs were found. Our prophets are resting under Moslem shrines with crescents over their heads. The Moslems believe that Abraham was their prophet, a Moham-medan and an Arab, and refuse to believe that he was a Hebrew. Apparently we all own Abraham. We saw Abraham's oak, such a big tree; Paul looked wee standing beside it. The tree is nearly dead, and certainly looks as though it might be four thousand years old; its remaining branches are propped up with big irons.

A funny old Arab carried Paul all over the mosque, but Paul didn't mind. I am sure he will think England is awfully dull with no funny men in bright orange turbans and yellow cloaks.

2nd July

We can't make any definite plans. The Governor has gone to England with precise instructions that Cliff mustn't leave until he comes back, and he has a habit of wangling an extra month when he gets to England. I don't want to come alone if I can help it: it seems such a waste, doesn't it, when it would spoil the voyage for us both if we came separately? But I don't want to keep Father and Mother waiting. I am afraid they will be very cross with me for not booking berths long ago. I am getting thoroughly Eastern and Cliff is developing the patience of Job.

I am reading the Old Testament as a novel, and finding it intensely interesting, but I feel less and less like treating it as a God-given inspiration: Abraham and his family are so like wily old Bedus.

There is a strike on in Jerusalem: taxi drivers with most of the gharry men out in sympathy. The gharry drivers that haven't gone on strike are making fortunes by charging double fares. The strikers are so annoyed that they killed one man's horse yesterday.

7th August

I don't think I ever told you that I had an Armenian woman and her daughter (aged about fourteen). I have had them for over three months now, and they seem satisfactory. The mother is very good and loves Paul; she does the cooking and cleans, and the daughter, called Elainie, looks after Paul and takes him for walks in the afternoons. The mother, Sarohiae, is a widow with a good-for-nothing son and five daughters. The oldest daughter was married last week, and we were invited to the wedding. It was such a queer ceremony. We were invited for eight o'clock on a Sunday evening, and the bride lives in the Armenian quarter of the old city, so we had to go down all sorts of weird passages and narrow streets before we came to the house. We were shown into a small room, fairly full of people. On one side was a divan where the bride was sitting looking very beautiful in white silk and lace, orange blossom and net veil all complete. She was much perfumed and powdered. In front of the bride stood two small children in white, each holding a huge decorated candle, and between them stood a perfectly sweet little bridesmaid of three years old, carrying a nosegay. We were given the place of honour by the bride, and regaled with banana liquor and Arabic cakes whilst two men played and sang Arabic music. We sat like this for an hour whilst the room got fuller and fuller. Everyone saluted the bride as they came in by kissing her on both cheeks. She looked very miserable, and I felt sorry for her until I learned that it is very infra dig for a bride to smile on her wedding day! At 9 o'clock the bridegroom's party arrived, and we all set off in procession for the church. It must have looked very romantic to see us in those old picturesque streets, the priests in scarlet and gold, the white bride and the candles and the musicians. The ceremony in the church was rather a joke: the priest kept stopping in the middle to tell the people to be quiet, as everyone was talking. We could not understand the service, of course. The bride and bridegroom stood face-to-face with their foreheads touching, and a man held a little gold cross over them. When the service was over, we processed again, this time to the house. On the way, the bridegroom held the bride's arm on one side and mine – as the honoured guest – on the other. At the house, we drank coffee and ate more cakes, and listened to the women making awful caterwauls of joy, which we found rather heart-rending. We didn't get home until eleven, it was a most exciting evening.

13th August

I am very much surprised that you have not been receiving all my letters. I am rather distressed because one I sent was full of very important news, and that is that I am going to have a Lois (*baby girl*) in January or February next and I wrote asking your advice whether I should stay here or come home to have the baby. We have been thinking hard, with the result that Paul and I are coming home some time next month. Please send a cable. This letter may be really very thrilling to you, but I am so used to the idea of a family that my remarks may seem rather casual. Needless to say I am dying to see my next baby. I hope that Lill will be ready to make frocks et cetera. We decided that it wasn't fair to you not to see any of the babies.

27th August

The Governor came back last week and said that Cliff could not leave until the clock tower was finished. I have decided to come back with some pilgrims: there are about thirty of them staying here, mostly very nice women, and they are quite willing to take me under their wing, and to help me to look after Paul. I think that Sophie is coming to look after Cliff, and I hope he will be able to come home for Christmas.

The offending Turkish clock tower over the Jaffa Gate

4th October
To Mother from Gildersome, Cliff's home near Leeds
I cannot understand there not being a decent nursing home in Birkdale or Southport: it seems extraordinary, surely one must be possible. I think I shall go back to Jerusalem.

9th October
To Elizabeth, from Gildersome
I wish she (Mother) would not worry so, especially as there is nothing to worry about. I should just put the whole thing into Dr Wheeler's hands: after all it's his case. Anyway, I have decided to go back to Jerusalem as soon as possible. Cliff doesn't think he can come home for Christmas, and I can't risk being here without him for an indefinite period. The East is the East and nothing will hurry workmen there, so the clock tower may go up horribly slowly. I never intended her to upset herself like this. I can manage the whole thing perfectly well myself. I did it in Jerusalem. I do wish they wouldn't make me feel so ashamed of myself by talking about wearing corsets and buying lose clothes et cetera. It's so different in Palestine, where everyone is so pleased and interested and sane and open about it. No whispering in corners like the ghastly English attitude. No, I'm sure if I stayed here I shouldn't have a nice happy baby like Paul. Of course mother wouldn't understand all this, she thinks all my ideas are mad. If she didn't, she would consult me instead of planning with you about what is going to happen to me and Cliff.

I'm not sorry I came home. They have seen Paul, which is what I came for, but really I do feel as though I am upsetting the house dreadfully. Except Father: I know he is quite contented. And besides it has been a change. I have written to ask Cliff to come for me: I wish he could, just a month's leave, it would be fun.

Very many thanks for your letter and sympathy… No, I'm not worrying, and I only wish that Mother wasn't, but I am determined to go back to Jerusalem… Uncle Percy came this afternoon and took us for a drive – at my suggestion – and bought us some chocolates, also at my suggestion! He seems quite happy about it; liked my hair and hat and Paul, and wants to see us again before we go.

22nd November
Cliff to Elizabeth
In three weeks time, I shall be homeward bound. What excitement! Please don't thank me for letting Eunice come home: she did it on the spur of the moment, and we are both very sorry for it now. It won't happen again.

I've got many thrilling things to do next year. My private jobs will include a block of flats, a building for The Bible Society, and an extension to the Ophthalmic Hospital of the Order of St. John of Jerusalem.

6

1925

E unice was home for five months, during which time her second son John
was born. She left to return to Jerusalem in March. The friendly welcome,
the return to Beit Syriac and the start on new jobs for Cliff all indicate a more
settled life. Jerusalem itself was quiet, and the replacement of Sir Herbert
Samuel, a Jew, as High Commissioner by Lord Plumer was welcomed by the
Arabs. Although Jewish immigration was high in 1925, three thousand a month,
things were peaceful, and the authorities seem to have been lulled into a false
sense of security.

Although most of the immigrants settled in Tel Aviv and Kibbutz (agricultural villages) in the west of the country, some growth of population and activity
in Jerusalem must have encouraged the need for completion of the civic survey
and the preparation of a town plan for Jerusalem. The Governor and High
Commissioner seem to have been pleased with the survey, and the plan went
ahead, although apparently slightly delayed until space for an office was available
in the house.

In October, Eunice writes that she has been to Jaffa for the first time. This
is over three years since she arrived in Palestine, and shows the relative lack of
travel, as well as the absence of historical attraction in modern Jaffa. In fact, the
main reason for going seems to have been an invitation by Sir Ronald Storrs to
visit an exhibition of Palestine Industries in Tel Aviv, then a fast growing Jewish
town of over 30,000 population. Travel was not particularly easy, even though
distances were small. Roads were narrow, often unsurfaced and steep, besides
being unsafe. Cars were sometimes unreliable, with frequent punctures and
engine problems. The photograph of the Jerusalem to Jericho road gives some
idea of the country that had to be crossed.

3rd February
Rosleigh Nursing House, Southport
John born. The home is very nice, but boring beyond words compared with Jerusalem. Instead of a jolly succession of afternoon callers from about the third day on, and a most varied collection of babies to look at from the big ward, I'm relegated to one member of the family per day, and Winnie when she has time. Not to mention the fact that there is no lying in the garden and basking in the sun. Still, I'm surviving!

To Elizabeth from Stanley Avenue, Birkdale
Cliff has taken Paul to Gildersome this morning, so I can have a restful week. Paul went off with great glee at the prospect of a 'tar' and a 'puff puff'. John is an exceptionally good baby and Paul loves him. He treats him as a huge joke, and is not in the least jealous.

2nd April
From Jerusalem
We arrived at Port Said at 7.00 on Friday morning. We went to the Marina Palace Hotel and engaged a small room for the day. After that, we had the nine-hour journey to Jerusalem. It is now Sunday; Paul, Cliff and Ben Dor are playing with Paul's train, and an old Arab has just called, and is sitting on the floor entranced: he has never seen anything like it before. Ben Dor is Cliff's main office assistant.

14th April
Many thanks for your letters and newspapers. We saw the picture of the Dome of the Rock which Balfour was not being allowed to visit. As a matter of fact, he did visit it because the Gendarmerie, dressed up as American tourists, took him there and showed him everything. It was very quiet there. All the Arabs shut their shops, and I saw one house draped in black; otherwise there was no disturbance. Balfour seems to have had a very much worse time in Syria. They say that the Palestine Arabs had been talked to by their leaders, and persuaded not to do anything foolish.

Last night, Cliff and I went to Passover night service at the house of Ben Dor. It was all very interesting and symbolic. We ate the Matsa – unleavened bread – and bitter herbs, signifying the exile, a roasted egg, signifying the plenty of the promised land and slices of cucumber dipped in salt, which meant I've forgotten what! We had a large supper in the middle of the service, and afterwards all the company sang old Hebrew songs. There was present at the supper the Chief Rabbi of Rome: he sang songs and read beautifully. Of course they had the seven branched candlestick on the table.

The Bible Society representative came to dinner last night to study the plans. Four of the committee are coming from Port Said, and will come to tea tomorrow. The building should begin soon.

Cliff went to the opening of the University, and was bored to tears. He said that Balfour's speech was the only redeeming feature. The Rabbi spoke for so long that he had to be dragged away by the chairman.

28th April
Cliff has a new job, a hostel and memorial chapel: it is a Scottish Memorial, and the chapel is Presbyterian of course.

21st May
A fellaheen worker of Cliff's bought a present of a sheep for Paul, rather an embarrassing present. We decided to kill and eat it, as we couldn't keep a sheep in the garden indefinitely. So Grey (Sophie's husband) killed and skinned it one night. We didn't know how Paul would take the absence of 'baa', as he had been very fond of it. What happened was rather startling: Paul went into the kitchen and saw the sheep's head and feet in a bowl on the floor, but instead of being frightened, as I thought he would be, he ran to me laughing and saying, 'Loot, loot, baa broken'.

7th June
Cliff has nearly finished the drawings for the survey of Jerusalem. He has had a most hectic month, and he and Ben Dor are absolutely fagged. Cliff found a Roman mosaic floor last week: workmen were digging through it.

10th June
We are very excited, as Cliff made a big discovery yesterday, when he found the remains of a Jerusalem city wall, one there has been a lot of controversy about. It is over three metres thick, so it must be a city wall, the one built by Agrippa. The archaeologists are very excited about it. It is the most important thing that has been discovered for some time.

17th June
We are turning out Mrs Nixon next month from half her house, and taking it all over ourselves. Cliff is going to have two rooms for offices. I work there instead of at the Governorate, where his room is much too small. Also, I shall have a nursery.

27th June
We take over the whole house next month. The long-talked-of town plan will begin as soon as Cliff gets a room and a big table. The Civic Survey drawings are

very good. Storrs and Sir Herbert Samuel were very pleased with him. Not a word about John! His chief asset seems to be good-temperedness.

The water shortage is going to be rather serious this year. It's horrid to watch the flowers dying.

4th July

I am writing this in the interval between John's bottle and Paul's soup. Well, Sir Herbert Samuel went on Thursday, amid many farewells et cetera. There have been many celebrations, but we only went to a few of them.

I suppose you will now have heard about the new skull of the ape man that one of Garstang's students found in Galilee? It is very rare, the only one yet found in Asia: everyone is very excited about it. We are going to see it soon: it is at the British School until it goes to England.

23 August

Stern's mother and sister came round last night, and brought Paul a watering can, so he has been busy watering flowers all morning. We have had Government water put into the house, and are now the proud possessors of two taps, one in the kitchen and one in the bedroom. We also have a shower. Paul talked all last night about his 'candle water' and, after a terrible brain effort, I discovered that he meant watering can. The water isn't cold, because the pipe runs through the garden, where the sun shines on it.

Shops are being built near the house, and camels come all day long, carrying stones for building. When Paul hears the bells, he rushes to the window to watch them being unladened.

Plumer arrived yesterday; great excitement. All the Arabs are delighted, of course. He is just like his picture, large moustaches, rows and rows of medals et cetera, very military.

13th September

There are very few flowers here now. The Citadel gardeners bring me a nosegay every Saturday evening, and I make it last until the following Saturday. No-one has any water to spare for flowers. We are never actually short of water: we have a cubic metre tank, which fills up every other day with municipal water, and if we do use it all in two days (which has only happened once so far) we have a little cistern to fall back on (metaphorically speaking)... Please, what is rummy?

18th September

John is to be christened on Sunday in the Church of the Holy Nativity, Bethlehem. I wish you were here: why not fly over for the weekend? All the arrangements have been made, as of course it is a Greek church, and permission has to be obtained from the Greek Patriarch. We are going on Sunday afternoon in two cars: Mr Steer (the Bishop's Chaplin, who is christening John, for the Bishop is in England) and Mrs Steer; there will also be Mrs Cook and Sheila, Mrs Bomberg, Miss Key, Paul, Sophie, Cliff, John and me. So John will be christened in one of the oldest churches in the world, built by the first Christian Roman Emperor, Constantine.

23rd September
Sunday was a great success. We had to have both babies dressed and fed by three, all ready and the kettle on the stove, for both Sophie and Raoofie wanted to come. We arrived at half past three, and walked through the big church into a small chapel, where the christening took place. We sat in a row. Paul and Sheila stood and watched, wide-eyed. John talked, and wriggled the whole time, but did not cry once. When Mr Steer took him, he lay quite still and watched the yellow candlesticks over his head. Paul was very good until the last prayer, when he suddenly began to sing at the top of his voice 'Mary had a little lamb'. Greek priests were wandering about all through the service and, when it was over, the chief one took us all up to the very top of the building, where we sat in a room and were given the usual repast of queer-tasting pink drinks, chocolate biscuits and coffee.

3rd October
I went to Jaffa yesterday for the first time. Cliff and I (no babies) were invited to go with Sir Ronald and Lady Storrs and their daughter Mary. We started at 11.30 by car, ate sandwiches on the way and arrived at Tel Aviv, the Jewish part of Jaffa, at about 1.30, where we had to inspect an exhibition of Palestinian industries. Later, we went to the docks to visit the flag ship *Queen Elizabeth*, which is there this week. It is a beautiful ship, and we had a lovely time on board. Funnily enough, I had seen her before. Do you remember me going with Dr Tordof and Eileen when the ship was in the Mersey? Of course, we saw it much better this time, for the Captain showed us around and explained everything. We ended up with being entertained by the Admiral, having tea in his room, which is the room where the treaty for the handing over of the German fleet was signed. We saw the table where Beatty and the others sat, and a painting, by Lavery, of the event.

25th October
The town plan is being coloured, at last. We have waited for this day for months, it is a wonderful effort. This isn't the final plan, of course, just the development plan. Yesterday, Cliff and Professor Garstang, Dr Mayer (archaeologist) Pere Vincent (Dominican father) and another man all helping him to fix the antiquities sites. It is fun having the drawing office next to the house. Ben Dor

and another draughtsman (Harmat) sing duets, operas, national anthems, German student songs et cetera. Ben Dor knows 'My name is Dr Thomson Brown', Dormat (Harmat) only speaks about six words of English, but he sings 'God save the King' most lustily. He is a Hungarian Jew. Paul helps to draw sometimes; he is allowed to walk on the table if he takes his shoes off! I think we shall stay in this house as long as we stay in Jerusalem. It is the loveliest place, everyone adores it, and the garden is marvellous for the babies. They are out all day long, from 7.00 in the morning. I don't know when we shall come home, or whether we shall stay here another year: it all depends on Cliff's jobs. There is much more chance of getting things to build here than in England. The house is much nearer the town than where we were in Nashashibi Corner, about 12 minutes from the Jaffa Gate.

13th November
I have been working on the town plan for a week. It is to be finished today. Sir Ronald returns from Cairo this morning, and expects to see it finished. I have just finished my job, colouring roads.

From Cliff
We are all feverishly excited about the town plan: three solid months' work, besides stacks of previous research. You will be thrilled at the size of it if nothing else: 10 feet by 10 feet.

November
Now the rain has come, we are caring for our garden. I am going to keep hens and grow vegetables. We have been having Jewish boy scouts to come and work in the garden, doing odd jobs to make money for their scouts, and they are going to make me a hen-run and dig.

The YWCA bazaar was quite a big affair. I helped Lady Storrs with her stall with Mrs Brooks (Lady Plumer's daughter) and a Miss Gate. I helped to arrange the stall all morning and sold in the afternoon. Miss Gate and I were there at 2.00 to sell to the Moslem ladies, who came from 2.00 to 3.00 as, of course, they could not come when the men were there. The bazaar made nearly £300.

22nd December
I went to a dance at the Allenby: they have one every Saturday night. There, there is a very black man called Mr Dudley, who conducts the jazz band and is very gay and entertaining.

7

1926

I mpressions of a stable family life in a trouble-free Jerusalem grow in this year. The children take up more time, a car is bought, Eunice's sister Elizabeth comes out from England for a second time. She finds the house full of activity, family and office work, and shared exploits. At work, the town plan was presented to the Jewish and Arabic press, and Cliff completed drawings of what was to be the first of three Barclay's Bank buildings in Palestine.

Eunice writes for the first time about the Sea of Galilee, which was then a quiet and idyllic place. We stayed at a German Hospice in Tabgha, right on the shore and run by a gentle and friendly Father Tepper. It was near the traditional site of the miracle of the loaves and fishes. Tiberias and Capernaum were also nearby, the former once the centre of Jewish Palestine after the destruction of the Temple in AD 70, and where scholars preserved the identity of Judaism.

The Crusades get little mention in the correspondence, but the moving of the tombstone of Philip d'Aubigny in the precincts of the Holy Sepulchre was an important matter, mentioned by Sir Ronald Storrs in his autobiography[3]. This was the only surviving tombstone of a crusader, and needed to be moved if the inscription was to be saved from wear and tear. The tomb had to be opened and a new grill, designed by Cliff, put over the stone. Any interference with the structure of the Holy Sepulchre was fraught with religious difficulties and, as Storrs describes it, 'the surrounding roofs, terraces and battlements were thronged with black-stoled Greek Caloyers (monks) to witness the event'. As an agnostic, Cliff had another occasion to demolish a small piece of the wall of the Holy Sepulchre which was thought to be of both structural concern and historic interest.

Eunice's sister Elizabeth arrived in August with a friend, Eleanor Hollinshead. Her letters are most enthusiastic about the house and household, containing as it did Cliff's office staff during the day, Ben Dor and Harmat being the backbone and often accompanying the family on outings. One of these outings was a moonlight picnic to the Dead Sea, which was obviously very much enjoyed. Elizabeth also enlarges on the charms of the Wadi Kelt, mentioning the beautiful green Wadi with date palms and bananas in full fruit, and the need to hire a donkey for the steep climb back.

The first car was bought in the summer, a second-hand Renault. From the letters it is apparent that Eunice drove, which is counter to all I heard in later life, when she said she never had done. My own recollection is that she was made to drive once when the car got stuck in the sand. On this occasion Cliff was pushing and Eunice put the car into reverse!

Strangely enough, Eunice nowhere refers to the departure of Sir Ronald Storrs in this year, when he left to become Governor of Cyprus. He had clearly played an important part in their lives, with encouragement and friendship in the early days. As a founder member of the Pro-Jerusalem Society, and with Cliff as Secretary, there had been a close and successful working relationship. An invitation to visit him in Cyprus followed his departure, and Storrs visited Cliff and Eunice both in Jerusalem and later in England.

16th January

Yesterday Cliff gave an hour's talk on the town plan to representatives of the Jewish press. Today he gives the same talk to the Arabs. This morning, he has gone with Sir Ronald Storrs to inspect a proposed site for the new Government House. The moving of the crusader was an interesting thing to do. Philip d'Aubigny was a crusader, also a governor of the Channel Islands, a tutor to Henry? (I've forgotten which) and the first man to sign the Magna Carta after King John. He came to Jerusalem later on a pilgrimage; died here of the plague,

Lowering the tombstone of the crusader Philip d'Aubigny outside the Holy Sepulchre

Cliff at the tomb of Philip d'Aubigny

and was buried in front of the Holy Sepulchre door. Up until about 1850, the place of his tombstone was covered by a platform where the Moslem tax-gatherers sat. When the taxes were abolished, the platform was moved and there was the tomb underneath. Now to prevent it being worn away by people's feet, Sir Ronald got money from the crusader's descendants (who still live in the Channel Islands) and has had it taken up and lowered below the level of the pavement, and a grille put over it which Cliff designed.

We went to a Bohemian supper at the Bombergs this week, and had a lovely time. We ate hors d'oeuvres, soup, pigeons, baked potatoes and peas, cheese and biscuits, cakes and coffee. It was all cooked on two primus stoves. We sat on stools and ate the pigeons with our fingers, as there weren't enough knives to go around. They have just sold some paintings, hence the revelry!

14th February

We are staying at the most heavenly place you can possibly imagine: Tabgha, where there is this old German Hospice kept by a delightfully affable German Father who has been here for years. The house is on the north shore of the Sea of Galilee, so we have a view right down the lake. I am sitting on a verandah from which I can see the house; it is an old black and white stone building covered in front with a creeper which is a blaze of bright magenta flowers, Bougainvillia. Just in front is a grove of orange trees full of fruit, and in front of the house there are several beautiful palm trees. Crowds of white doves keep flying round and round above my head. Beyond the garden is the lake, as blue as the sky, and on the other side are the hills of Transjordan. The weather is glorious, just like the best kind of English summer day, and the lake and surrounding country reminds me very much of the Lake District at home. There has been just enough rain to cover the hills with green, so that the man who wrote about 'the fair green hills of Galilee' doesn't seem to be quite so daft as we thought him two years ago. It is a little too early for the flowers, but there are some red anemones out. About three minutes' walk away is a stream coming from a warm spring, so we swim hard in the cold sea and then lie in the warm stream, it's lovely! It's joy to have Sophie here to look after Paul and John in this lovely garden, and leave us free to wander about as we like. She took them this morning to see the fishermen bring in the fish, and Paul came back with three dead fish in his bucket which he is most anxious to eat. John finds pebbles the most fascinating toy, but Paul prefers fishes and ducks.

This afternoon we went to Tiberias, but it is a dreadful place. It is full of Jews and very dirty. The Arabs say that the king of fleas lives in Tiberias, and I can quite believe it. We walked to Capernaum the other evening, where there is an old ruin of a synagogue supposed to be the one in which Christ healed the centurian's servant; but present day archaeologists don't seem very certain about it. Anyway, it was a lovely walk by the shores of the lake.

12th March

We had a lovely time at the dance: Cliff got the first prize for his costume. People were amused as we were the only Christians there. Cliff's dress was very good. He had three wolf skins for the main garment, his arms and legs were painted brown, and he wore a red ragged wig. He stuck on projecting eyebrows with pink putty and wore sandals and a necklace of shells on leather. He carried a club and a lovely flint on a wooden handle. The prize was a beautiful book on Russian art, Pasternak. We danced hard and went to bed about four in the morning.

I have lost Sophie: she had to go back to her husband. There is no law here to help her, and as he decided he wanted her back, she had to go.

18th March

This week, some members of the Order of St John of Jerusalem have been here on a pilgrimage. There were over a hundred of them, and some very important people amongst them. Cliff had to go with Sir Ronald on Sunday afternoon to take them round the city walls, and also on Tuesday to show them Solomon's quarries. They had a big reception at the Opthalmic Hospital on Tuesday, to which we were invited. All the knights of the order were in their robes, a black gown with a large star embroidered on one side and a round black velvet hat. We were received by the Earl of Scarborough, who was interested in Cliff because he had seen the town plan, which is still hanging on the wall of the Governor's room. There was one lovely lady who looked as if she had stepped out of a

Gainsborough picture. She had a large black hat with a feather on top, and to one side of her head and underneath were masses of grey wavy hair: and she looked as if she might have had two ringlets over one shoulder. The 'picture' was completed by a feather boa and a bunch of violets. I think she was the Countess of Airlie. Lady Beatty was there, and looked very nice.

7th April

On Monday, we went to Tel Aviv for the day. Tel Aviv is a very new part of Jaffa, completely Jewish and very modern. It has mostly been built since the war. Its architecture is extraordinary. It was lovely to see the sea. In the afternoon we went to the Tel Aviv Exhibition, and Cliff bought me a lovely batik scarf and sunshade. We picked up Ben Dor and Harmat and brought them home… Mrs Taylor's letters where interesting to read. Please tell her to come to Jerusalem as there are crowds of Jewish communists here. Palestine is full of them.

A sad thing happened here last week. Mrs Chaikin (whose baby you made a coat for) had another baby just a month ago. A week after the birth, she got ill, and she died last week. We were very upset. The husband is Cliff's best friend out here. He is an oldish man – she was my age – and is left with these two little sons: one twenty months and one nearly a month. Isn't it dreadful? Everyone seems to think it was the hospital's fault; she was in a very strict Jewish hospital, and the doctors don't seem to known what was the matter.

16th April

I suppose you know that Princess Mary has been. I have seen her twice. Once at the Holy Fire and then at the Armenian feet-washing ceremony. She is much smaller and much prettier than I had thought her to be. I enclose a card for the Bible House opening. Cliff has been given a very nice Bible. Ben Dor and Harmat have been given Bibles in Hebrew.

17th April

We had a lovely day on Sunday. We went to visit the Bombergs, who are staying at Wadi Kelt. This is the deep valley near Jericho where Elijah was fed by ravens; where John the Baptist lived and preached and where hundreds of hermits have lived ever since. We could see their little caves – just like holes – high up in the rocks. It's a terribly steep valley, the rocks are tremendous and wonderfully shaped. On the side of the valley is a convent where the Bombergs have been lent a room. Apparently there are only two monks there, both more or less mad: one is Greek, the other Russian. The convent is very clean and most picturesque, and has a beautiful little green garden. There is a spring and a pool with lots of lovely moss and maidenhair. We went in a car to the top of the valley, taking Ben Dor, Harmat and Paul with us. Then we had to climb down the steep side to the bottom, where we discovered Bomberg painting, and Mrs Bomberg holding the brushes, so to speak. We prepared lunch under a big cliff. Luckily we had taken plenty of provisions, for Mrs Bomberg was absolutely out of stock. They had nothing but a tin of bully beef, one of baked beans and some funny little scones Mrs B. had baked on a primus... We had a great feed, and then walked to the pool, where Ben Dor and Harmat had a swim; Mrs B., Paul and I paddled while Cliff and Bomberg talked art. It was a glorious day.

23rd May
We have had a wireless for two nights. Mr Pierce has it on trial and, as he was bored with it in his bedroom at the Hospice, brought it here. The first night, we heard Big Ben at one in the morning!

Eunice with Paul

Left to right: David and Alice Bomberg, Ben Dor, unknown, Paul, Harmat, Eunice

Jerusalem, looking towards the Holy Sepulchre, oil
by David Bomberg, 1925

19th June

Paul had a cold shower this morning: he loved it. Of course the water is on the
roof in a zinc cistern, and exposed to the sun from about 4 o'clock in the
morning, so the water isn't really cold. We get up at 6.30 every morning, and
Cliff is at the office at 7.30. I'm working there too this week as Cliff has to get
the bank plans finished by Wednesday afternoon; so, as usual, we are in a rush.
We got fed up one night, and went to the circus. There is a travelling circus near
our house, from Hungary (much to Harmat's delight) and really quite good. As
I'd never been to a circus before, I was curious and interested. The horses were
glorious; great big shining things. You should have seen the old Arabs in kafiehs
and abbayas enjoying themselves. The circus was conducted in Arabic, Hebrew,
German, English and French, all very badly: Cliff said so badly that he could
understand everything they said! Languages are funny here... I rang up the
plumber yesterday and, as I couldn't understand what he said, I called Ben Dor.
Ben Dor said 'Are you speaking Hebrew, Arabic, German or English?' The
answer was 'Español'. After that, he gave up. We don't rise to Spanish in the
office.

26th June

I have been working in the office all week, and have done little else but draw. The plans for Barclay's Bank had to be ready yesterday, and we have been going full speed. We don't yet know whether the building will go up; it is to be combined with the municipal offices, a big building on an important site, right in the centre of the town... Cliff is absolutely fed up with the Bible Society. They are terrible people to deal with, who don't seem to know their own minds, and who at the same time won't trust anyone in Jerusalem to advise them. Cliff would like to give up the job altogether, it's so disheartening, but as they owe him over £400, we feel he had better stick to it.

8th August

We have just heard that the Bible Society building is to go up at last. I am so glad and, the Society having paid up part of the fees, we are thinking of buying a second-hand car.

13th August

Elizabeth and her friend Eleanor Hollinshead arrived, looking as neat and tidy and fresh as though they had each come out of a bandbox. They have settled down and seem to be happy here. This afternoon we went on a pilgrimage. We started to walk up the Via Dolorosa to see the Stations of the Cross, and half way we caught up with an Italian pilgrimage, so we added ourselves on to the end and followed along to the Holy Sepulchre. The pilgrims were a collection of Italian priests and nuns, Franciscans and Arab women, and were led by an Italian Cardinal.

19th August.

Today being Thursday, and Nanny's day off, we had another badminton day. Elizabeth is completely dazed by all the odd people who seem to congregate here. There is a boy who is teaching Cliff to drive his car and Kamarof, who is the Pro-Jerusalem Society gardener and the painter (not that he plays with us, but Elizabeth mixes him up with the other people).

We intended to have a small dance tonight, but two of our guests didn't come, so we were a very small party. However, we danced hard. Harmat gave us tango lessons, and Elizabeth learned steps to teach the Captain of the Massilia when she goes home. We sang songs between whiles, and one of them was the Red Flag. When we stopped, we heard someone whistling it outside, but when we looked out of the window we could only see two policemen looking at the house, and writing in a notebook. Elizabeth has been expecting Cliff to be arrested all day as a dangerous communist.

25th August

Elizabeth has told you of all our moonlight picnics. We had our most exciting one last night. We spent the night on the shores of the Dead Sea. We left here at 5.30 last night. Elizabeth and Eleanor having become very friendly with Ben Dor and Harmat, we asked them to join our excursion. The Russian (whose name we have all learnt now) Dolgenski drove a hired car, so we were seven in the party. The drive was lovely, with the setting sun making the hills all pink. By the time we got to the Dead Sea, it was quite dark. We found the shore inhabited by a Bedouin tent with Bedus complete, a few empty barracks, a very small hotel and a Jewish friend of Ben Dor's who is doing experiments in salt down there. We sat by the sea on the pebbles and waited for the moon to rise. It came quickly over the Mountains of Moab and made everything very light and the sea all silvery. There was a small wooden platform half over the sea which we chose for our picnic place. We had a big supper, salad, salmon, ham, eggs, pudding, nuts, chocolate. We felt quite replete afterwards, so we had a little rest before bathing. By this time, the moon was well up, so we prepared for a bathe. The usual procedure is to vaseline oneself all over in case of scratches or spots which would hurt in the salt water, but Elizabeth doubted the need for vaseline and just greased half of herself to test it. The water is most queer. Elizabeth said it was just her kind, for she couldn't possibly sink. It's a lovely feeling to walk in the water. We licked our fingers, and they tasted terribly bitter and salty. When we came out, someone remarked that we should feel just like sardines in a tin, well greased and salty. After our bathe we went to the room of Ben Dor's friend and had Russian tea and biscuits. He offered his room with two small beds to Elizabeth and Eleanor for the night. Cliff and I settled ourselves on blankets on the pebbles right on the shore, Ben Dor and Dolgenski a little further on, and Harmat on the platform. It was a glorious night, and we slept well outside. Elizabeth had a wonderful sleep, but Eleanor didn't, so she was up first. We others woke at dawn, just in time to see the sunrise. It was quite too wonderful to describe: the mountains, queer and weird in the daytime, are even queerer when they are pink and green. Elizabeth collected some plants before breakfast, and by the time we started back it was getting very hot. We went home by way of Jordan and Jericho, and arrived here at 10.00 this morning. Eleanor had a sleep, and we have all washed off the salt and feel most well and happy... Paul discovered his heart beating this morning, and wanted to know what he had a little heart for.

27th August

Today was the feast of the Virgin Mary. It is a great fantasia held all round the Church of St Mary's Tomb. We went to it this afternoon: the hillside was covered with people all in the brightest coloured dresses; they were having picnics, some of them in tents, some under trees. We went in the church and saw a shrine of St Mary, under which women were crawling, passing their babies in order to get a blessing.

We had thought of another moonlight picnic tonight, but when we found that it meant a four hour donkey ride, we decided otherwise.

10th September

We can hardly believe that Elizabeth and Eleanor will be going in less than a week. We have had such a lovely time, and we shall miss them very much. We are making the most of our last few days. We visited Hebron yesterday. I think that I have described it to you before, the big mosque built over the Cave of Macpelha, where Abraham, Sarah, Isaac, Jacob, Rebecca and Leah are lying, Joseph just outside. Whether their bodies are actually there or not, nobody knows. The cave was opened up five hundred years ago, and has been closed ever since.

We have had a mosque week. We saw the Dome of the Rock and the Aksa Mosque on Wednesday. It is a gorgeous place. I haven't been in since my first week in Jerusalem. We were lucky enough to find Solomon's stables open, and went down. They consist of a most enormous room underneath part of the Temple area; the roof is supported by great arches on piers which make long arcades. The place is huge. Whether Solomon built it or not we don't know, but it is certainly very old.

Letters from Elizabeth in Jerusalem: second visit, August/September 1926

11th and 13th August

Here we are at last. This house is beautiful. It will be quite impossible to describe all its beauty and charm. The bedrooms, sitting room, nursery, large hall, and wonderful white bathroom are all above ground, and down either of two outside staircases are dining room and kitchen.

14th August

Cliff bought a second-hand Renault yesterday for £80. It is smaller than the Renault I have my eye on, but will easily take Cliff, Eunice and John at the front, and Nanny and Paul in the back. We are all going to learn to drive it, as though there were not enough excitement in Jerusalem already.

My indisposition is somehow or other the result of a visit to Jericho yesterday. Eunice and Eleanor think it is because I ate up all the cucumber sandwiches so that I could have the tin for specimens! It may of course have been the specimens themselves – 'Apples of Sodom' or Dead Sea fruit – a terrible sinister plant growing on the strange creviced floor of the Jordan Valley. The leaves look so green and juicy, and they are full of latex. The fruit is large and looks succulent and is full of air... we dropped three thousand feet in about one and a half hours... It is terribly weird country we passed through; I wouldn't like to fall among thieves there.

Oh, this is the most exciting household I have ever lived in. I'm not altogether clear yet as to precisely how many compose the household, but this afternoon (Nanny's day off) there are Ferideh and Eraz in the kitchen, Eunice and Eleanor and I playing badminton with Harmat, Ben Dor and Hadawi – four at a time – Ben Dor sometimes helping Cliff and Do (the Russian whose name I've forgotten and can't bear to go back and find now!) putting the car to rights.

24th August

We have had two wonderful picnics. The first was an all-day picnic to Wadi-el-Kelt (the Brook Kerith). We set off by car early, nine of us including Paul and Douglas Broadbent, a boy of about thirteen. We took the road to Jericho, and some way beyond the Good Samaritan Inn, we packed up our food, drink bathing suits, towels, ground sheet, mosquito net for Paul, and sent the car away. We then made our way down the rocky path to the beautiful green wadi, where

Wadi Kelt

At Wadi Kelt, left to right: Elizabeth, Cliff, Eunice, Douglas Broadbent(?), Harmat, Ben Dor

The Jerusalem-Jericho road

date palms and bananas were in full fruit. It was something of a disappointment to find our bathing pool – in a wild and trackless part of the wilderness of Judea – occupied by Arab schoolboys encamped there for the weekend. However, we settled down 'in the shadow of a great rock' for the day: bathing, eating and lazing. It was amazing how the day sped by. Cliff found a bottle of beer in a crevice of the rock, where he had left it six weeks before! At 6 o'clock we retraced our steps uphill, and it was heavy going. Half way up we hired a donkey and put on it all the burdens, including Paul! The Arabs who lent us the donkey supplied us (for a consideration, of course) with a great bunch of dates freshly cut from the tree. The bunch was so heavy I could hardly lift it. We were a goodly procession: in front Ben Dor leading the donkey and encouraging Paul to stick on, the Arab boy whipping it from behind. Then came Cliff, Eunice, Eleanor, Douglas, Harmat and then me, carrying the great bunch of dates slung on a pole. We felt like Joshua's spies returning from the land of milk and honey. It was a glorious moonlight night.

So, the following night we had a moonlight picnic to Ain Farah, the scene of the twenty-third psalm. It is another lovely wadi, the waters of which are now being brought to Jerusalem. It was really more like a canyon, and the road to it was terribly steep, with many hairpin bends. There are three pumping stations on the way down: it was amusing to see 'Mather and Platt Manchester' stamped on their engines. We ran into one of Ben Dor's many Arab acquaintances, who helped us carry our luggage to a nice round bathing pool. He was a shepherd, and he and four other shepherds and a little fellaheen girl sat round and watched us bathe by moonlight; they melted away before we had our picnic. It was all too beautiful to describe.

31st August

Since I wrote, we have been over the Hebrew University. Mr Lowry, the engineer and manager, showed us over it. It is small yet, but there are great plans ahead. Did you know that Einstein was coming as Professor of Mathematics or Physics? They have built a great outdoor lecture theatre on the side of the hill: it's like an amphitheatre. They have found an old tomb in the garden in which are several osaris, a kind of small stone sarcophagus for burnt remains of cremated bodies. It is probably Jewish, and about eight hundred years old. We have seen a lot of tombs, the Tombs of the Kings, and the Tombs of the Judges. On our way back, we walked through a settlement of Bokharian Jews, perhaps fifty or sixty years old. It was their Sabbath, and the women were wearing rich silk clothes and beautiful shawls over their heads. The men wear a kind of Astrakhan fez... We had a competition the other night as to how many types of headdress we had seen in Jerusalem, and we got to about forty, counting European hats as one.

You asked us what we did on Sundays. Well, last Sunday, we caught six hundred mosquitoes. We had a plague of them; they must have bred in one of the cisterns. We are enquiring into the matter now. Eunice supplied us each with a small vessel – a wineglass or egg-cup – with a little paraffin at the bottom. We quietly placed it under the mosquito on the ceiling, and it dropped in, overcome by the fumes. We all took part, and caught about 100 each.

I might have mentioned that in between the mosquito games on Sunday, Eleanor, Eunice and I went to the Church of St Anne. It is the most beautiful church in Jerusalem (Crusader).

Letters from Eunice

20th September

Yesterday, I had my first driving lesson. I drove from the Mufti's house to Tor village and back again. It was much nicer than I had expected.

22nd December

We had the Bible House stone-laying this afternoon. It was quite a success. Cliff wore his gown, and let the stone down on a chain while Lord Plumer laid it. There were quite a lot of people there, including Copts, Abyssinians, Armenians and Greeks.

I enclose a programme of Kubelik's concert: we liked it very much, but the general verdict seems to have been that he had much technique, but no soul. He gave four encores.

Christmas Eve

We are definitely leaving on 8th January by *Hector*, Blue Funnel Line. We shall come home overland from Marseilles, and so should arrive in London somewhere about the 15th. We are getting so excited.

It is 10 o'clock, and everyone is in Bethlehem except Paul, John and me: even Ferideh and Iraz have gone. Webb is here for Christmas and very much wanted to go, so Cliff has taken him. Nanny has never been, so she too is off with the YWCA people. Cliff and Webb took Ben Dor, and when Harmat arrived with a parcel, he too wanted to go, so all four squashed into the Renault and went off in high glee! The Jews, of course, wanted to see a Christian fantasia.

Harmat brought a huge tin of foie gras which came from Hungary. Ben Dor gave us some Italian leather work. We've had lots of presents this year. Ohenessian – the pottery man – sent us a basket of oranges, all of which had leaves on, and one had four huge oranges on one stock.

I shocked Cliff last night by dancing at the Bristol Garden. Harmat was there, and we did a tango. It was nearly an exhibition dance! Mr Dudley beamed at us.

We had a lovely Christmas. Fourteen people at tea: all of the office staff, Harmat, Ben Dor, Raphael, Mr Cornfelt, his wife and little baby, Miss Radinsky and her fiance, Webb from Cairo and the five of us. Webb stayed for dinner and another man came. Our Jerusalem turkey was beautiful, and so was the Yorkshire plum pudding… Cliff has gone to Cairo on Bible Society business with Mr Buchanan. I can't believe we leave here in nine days.

8

1927

D uring 1927 Eunice and Cliff had been in Jerusalem for five years, and one senses the change from a short-term adventure into the unknown to a settled long-term stay. The house was a more permanent one, and Cliff's work was changing its nature. Perhaps the departure of Sir Ronald Storrs and his winding up of the Pro-Jerusalem Society marked the closure of a post-war period, with a settling down of the Mandate, and less urgency of work on the old city. Cliff's job as Civic Advisor was also coming to an end, and he was to take up a new appointment the following year.

The household was joined by the appointment of Miss Cosen, later referred to as Bill, to help look after the children, and the office staff was increased to five, so that when the Bible Society building was finished this year the office moved in. A new job for Cliff was an extension to the Opthalmic Hospital, and this year the foundation stone of the Scottish Memorial Church was laid by Lord Allenby on the 7th May. The laying was a big occasion, and the church is the best known building by Cliff in Jerusalem.

Work on the church was held up when in July there was a fairly severe earthquake which caused damage in Jerusalem, Nablus, Lydda and Ramleh. The German Hospice on the Mount of Olives, which housed the High Commissioner, was severely damaged, and there was damage to the new University on Mount Scopus. Many buildings in the old city were also hit, and Cliff spent long hours on inspections of the damage, including some to his own house. In Nablus, seventy people were killed and some of the town was in ruins. Lydda was the site of the airport, and the first civil aviation flights, by Imperial Airways, operated from there this year.

In August, Eunice writes of staying in the German Hospice on Mount Carmel in Haifa, with its fine views over the sea. This was to be a favourite place to stay over the years, visited more frequently in the 1930s when the port and oil terminal were expanding and Cliff worked with Professor Abercrombie on the foreshore reclamation scheme.

In November, Eunice writes that they are moving heaven and earth to get home for Christmas, but they never did get there, for they had 22 people for tea in Jerusalem on Christmas Day.

The first three months were spent on leave in England.

26th April

I've had the most hectic time since we arrived. We had an easy journey up, with sleepers on the train. We expected to find Ben Dor at Batir, and there he was with a large bunch of flowers in his hand. Unfortunately, the train did not stop, and poor Ben Dor was left on the station whilst we sailed through! Harmat, Cornfelt and Raphael were at Jerusalem to greet us, and help with the luggage. Paul and John knew them all, and Paul was very friendly. The house looked bedraggled, and I wasn't at all pleased with the way Feridieh had kept it. She is getting slack, so I am giving her notice on Saturday. She will weep incessantly until she leaves, but I can't make her tidy, and it's demoralising to have an untidy maid and an untidy kitchen.

We like Miss Coe (Miss Cosen, a new governess). Paul came to me one day and whispered, 'Miss Coe climbed a tree'. He was full of admiration, and next morning asked her to repeat the performance; she refused, as Harmat was working at the office window. Soon she noticed Paul in deep conversation by the window; he came running back saying 'Harmat says he won't look'.

7th May

Today is a hectic day, as it is the Scottish Memorial stone laying. Cliff and Ben Dor have just gone off in the Renault carrying a table, the model, a suitcase with Cliff's gown etc. and two rugs for the platform. They were calling for the foundation stone on the way. The stone was laid by Field Marshall Allenby.

13th May

Someone has presented Cliff with a puppy, a two-month-old Saluki. He is one of those tall thin greyhound looking dogs. We have two dogs now, and I bathed them both one day. The puppy is very beautiful, a pure breed and quite valuable, but he is too ladylike for me. I prefer Simboul... I am just beginning to feel settled down. My new maid Vera, who is Russian, is still unintelligible, but she has stopped floor washing and seems quite bright.

I am enclosing a form of service for the stone laying. The Scottish ceremony was very simple and pleasing. We took Paul and John, who were both moderately quiet. The afternoon service doesn't seem to have been so successful. I liked it, but was not near enough to hear the speeches, which was very disappointing. There have been bitter complaints from ex-servicemen who were not invited.

Cliff has a new job. Alterations and a big wing to the Opthalmic Hospital of the Knights of St John. The hospital is opposite to where the Scottish Memorial will be.

1927

20th May

On Tuesday, I left my family and spent a day with Miss Buller in Ain Karim. It's a lovely little village, pretty little red roofed houses and tall cypress trees. The fields are full of olive, fig and apricot trees. I went by bus and Cliff, Coe and the boys called for me at six. I drove the car a little of the way home, but when I came to twelve donkeys that simply would not get out of the way, I got rather in a knot and retired from the wheel.

28th May

Cliff is contemplating buying a new car. We haven't quite decided yet, but we are going for a trial run this weekend. I'm driving the Renault as much as possible.

I drove a long way last night. I had both boys in the back seat and drove all through the town and into the back garden (Elizabeth will know what this means). Coe is now known as Bill: she has always been called Bill, and likes it better; so do I. We are still very satisfied with her.

We have a bear in Jerusalem, a big white woolly one which dances to a man playing a tambourine. Paul and John love it.

Excavations have been started again at Ophel. They have discovered part of a street with partly ruined houses on each side. They are complete with cisterns, a drainage system and mosaic floors - very little disturbed, the date supposed to be AD 500. It is remarkably well preserved and the pity of it is that it has all to be destroyed in order to see what is below. They hope to find the remains of David's Jerusalem beneath it.

11th June

Sophie is coming for the day on Mondays and Thursdays to take charge of the house, and I am going to have two days a week drawing in the office.

19th June

Miss Radinsky's wedding was very pretty. She looked lovely in white with a veil and orange blossom. The ceremony was simple enough, held on a big verandah in the bridegroom's house. The bridegroom was escorted under a sort of canopy held by four men. The bride came next with her father and mother; then she and her mother – followed by a bridesmaid – walked round the bridegroom seven times and then stood beside him whilst the Rabbi said prayers and sang. The Rabbi gave her wine to drink from a glass: this glass was then passed to the groom, who broke it with his foot. The ring was then put on, and the contract read by the Rabbi. All the men had to wear hats, including the bridegroom.

1st July
I registered Paul last week, so he is now a British subject and not a Palestinian any more.

9th July
The Bible House is going apace. Tomorrow, the roof will be finished, and always when the roof is on a building the workmen have a fantasia. So, tomorrow they stop work at eleven for a big feast. Two sheep are to be killed: they have been provided by Mr Buchanan.

15th July
I suppose that you have read about our earthquake? We were coming from Jaffa when it happened, and being in the car did not feel anything. There was great excitement when we got home: everybody was full of it. Our house swaying back and forwards (we have got two enormous cracks and several small ones). The children were in bed, and Bill in the garden, when it happened. She cried 'the children' and ran upstairs to find Sophie rocking herself on the bed crying 'Oh Jesus save us, oh Jesus save us.' So Bill said 'Come on Sophie, we'll do our bit', picked up the children and ran. Of course, by the time they got downstairs, it was all over. We got home at four, and Cliff went straight off with Cornfelt, Harmat and Shiffman to inspect the damage in the old city. Cliff said they visited about two hundred houses in all sorts of queer back places where he had never been before. All the poor people rushed out asking them if their houses were safe to sleep in. Shiffman estimated that about six hundred people slept in their beds who would otherwise have stayed out all night. They did not get home until nearly nine. Ben Dor came in and was recounting his adventures, and of course everybody talked at once... We had dinner at 10 o'clock. Cliff is going to Nablus tomorrow, and I may go with him. It is in a terrible state, half in ruins I believe. Cliff was terribly busy inspecting convents, banks, all sorts of buildings that are cracked. Government House is badly damaged and the Tower is likely to fall down any time. The University is also badly cracked. Everything on the Mount of Olives suffered. The top of the Minaret fell down and killed the old Sheik. The Bombergs were very upset. Bomberg had spent three weeks trying to get a certain roof to paint from, and he had just succeeded and done one morning's work, and it has fallen in. The Jews say he must be a very good man because God saved him by sending him down just before the earthquake... Well we have had no more shocks since Monday.

We went to Nablus. The destruction is terrible: it is not that the earthquake was bad there, but the houses were so very old that they could hardly hold together anyway. One suq was just a mass of stones, and we could see how badly the houses had been built. We found Mr Noble with what he called his 'dynamiter': he was blowing up houses that were too unsafe to remain. The number of dead on Saturday in Nablus was seventy, but there were more to dig out of the ruins.

22nd July

Cliff had to go to Salt in Transjordania yesterday to inspect the CMS hospital which is cracked. I went too. It is a lovely run and, on the way, we went to see the hotel in Jericho which has only been built one year. The construction was so bad that half of it is completely destroyed; all the furniture, beds, chairs, tables et cetera are all crumpled up amongst the stones, and everything is in a heap on the ground. Three Indian women were killed there: they were travelling on a pilgrimage and staying there a few days... Transjordan is much greener than Palestine; the road runs through a river bed which is beautifully green and full of oleanders covered with lovely pink bloom. The Jordan Valley, as we came back, was like an oven, misty, dusty and with a hot wind blowing up from the Dead Sea.

The Bible House is nearly finished, and much admired by all sorts of people. One day, an old Jew stopped Cliff and asked if he was the architect of the building. Cliff said he was, and that it was the Bible Society building. Then the old man said 'I think it is as beautiful as a Bible'. Wasn't that nice?

7th August

Cliff went up to Nablus again last week. It has been arranged to put lots of corrugated iron sheds outside the town as temporary dwellings for the poor people whose houses were destroyed. They will look hideous, of course, and be horribly hot in the summer and cold in the winter, but it seems to be the only thing to be done until some sort of a town plan has been made and there is money to build the houses.

Cliff has some funny experiences. Last week he had to arbitrate between the Syriacs and Armenians. It seems that the Armenians owned a room on top of the Syriac room (a queer arrangement, but probably dating back to centuries ago). In the earthquake, the Armenian room fell down but the Syriac room stood up. The Syriac thought it a good idea to get their room pulled down, so that they could henceforth own the land and the Armenians have no share. Unfortunately, their room was uncracked, so they hired two workmen to come with crowbars and make a hole in it in the middle of the night. But the Armenians had spies watching, and gave them away! Next, they offered the inspector £10 bakshish to say that the room was in a dangerous condition; but he happened to be an honest man and refused the bribe. Now it is left for Cliff and Chaikin to decide.

Cliff may be getting a job in Beirut. The English started to build a church there before the war and had to stop when the war broke out. The walls were only two feet high. Now they want to go on building, or begin a new one. Cliff hopes the latter, of course.

23rd August

Yesterday, Cliff had to go to Jaffa, so he combined business with pleasure and took Bill and me and the babies. Ben Dor came too, who had to help Cliff. They had to see some land at Lydda, where the temporary huts of those stricken by the earthquake are going to be. We went in the Renault, and left Ben Dor to follow on a motor bike. Unfortunately, it broke down, so he got a lift in a car. For the rest of the journey he sat on the side of the Renault! Of course part of the road was closed – it always is – and we had to go on a side track inches deep in sand, and of course we got stuck. Then I had to steer whilst the other three pushed! We finally had our picnic on the shore at Tel Aviv, far away past the town where it was beautifully clean and fresh. The children absolutely revelled in it.

26th August

We are going to Haifa for a holiday. We are staying at the German Hospice on Mount Carmel. Cliff will go to Beirut for two days with Mr Noble... I drove up the Mount of Olives, but unfortunately I ran over a stone and got a puncture, so Cliff drove home. I have not had a lesson since!

Here we are right up on the top of Mount Carmel, with a most heavenly view of the bay. The sea is a wonderful blue, the sand very white, and there are palm trees in the foreground. The slopes of Carmel are covered with pine trees. I wish you could all be suddenly transplanted here: you would love it, I am sure. It's ideal to be so high up and yet so near the sea. We came up on Thursday without a mishap. The little Renault pulled beautifully, and we hadn't even a puncture. We left Jerusalem at 10.30 and arrived here at 5.30. We had a picnic lunch outside Nablus. We spent Friday exploring Haifa shore. We found the bathing pool too smelly and too populated, so we all climbed in the car again and went to the left, round the point, but wherever we went was very rocky. We had a bathe at last, but the sea was so rough and the rocks so sharp that it wasn't exactly pleasant. In the afternoon, we went in the other direction towards Acre; it was really lovely there.

4th September

No, I don't feel like offering prizes to the Arabs to keep their donkeys clean: they would take the money and go off thinking what a silly fool I was.

1927

22nd September
To Elizabeth

Do you remember Kalta, the Jewish man who used to come and see Cliff? And do you remember the very bedraggled municipal garden in the Jaffa Road, beyond the clock tower that always looked very dull and deserted? Well, Kalta has put up an open-air cinema in the municipal gardens. It is a most attractive place, enclosed with a high wooden wall, painted blue and orange, and with jolly little electric lights all round: in fact, all the decorations are in blue, orange and black. At the back is a raised platform with comfy wicker chairs for the best seats. Kalta is trying to get only the best pictures, and we've been twice to see Douglas Fairbanks, once in the 'Thief of Baghdad' and once in 'Robin Hood'. Both were most amusing.

4th October

Cliff and Ben Dor are going up to Tiberias in the Renault. We have to hide Ben Dor here from sunset Wednesday evening, and they will leave early Thursday morning, because it is the Day of Atonement, and no Jew must ride in a car on that day, it's a most dreadful sin. They have to be careful not to stop at a Jewish place all the way there, in case he is discovered.

11th October

I've got Sophie back for three months, as her husband is in prison for debt, so if no-one pays up, there he will stay for three months. I hope he will stay, it will do him good and give Sophie a chance of earning a little money. Poor Sophie, she does have a terrible life. Sophie being here, Cliff and I, Bill and Ben Dor went a moonlight walk to the Citadel. It was locked, and there was no guard, so we were much exercised in how to get in. Finally, we slipped down the wall into the moat and walked along the moat garden trying to find a way into the Citadel itself. All we could find was a very small hole in a tower about two metres up. Ben Dor climbed up and found that it led into a room, so Bill and I were booted and pulled up and Cliff scrambled up after, so we all got in. We found various stoppages on the way, and had to push down some planks, but otherwise we were able to get in all the towers and see all the views. We made a big noise and rang all the Chinese bells, but no one heard us despite the fact that he police barracks were just next door! Cliff badly wanted to steal the little Chinese bell, because when Antiquities sent away old Ali because he was inefficient, Cliff said that if they put a police guard, he would steal a little bell to show how really efficient the police were. To get out, Ben Dor opened the lock with an iron bar (and locked it again) so that we could get back into the moat. We collected a rope which we used to slide down into the Jaffa Road; quite a large audience watching, of course!

14th October

We have been very busy this week moving Cliff's office from the house to the Bible Building. The offices are on the fourth floor and, as the lift is not in yet, it's no joke going up and down. Cliff has had his offices painted and distempered in very attractive, but rather staggering, colour schemes. It is a curious thing that none of the English people like the colours, but all the continentals absolutely rave about them. They love the brightness and modern atmosphere it gives.

9th November

We are moving heaven and earth to get home for Christmas, but I don't suppose we shall know until just before it is time to leave. There are so many people to consider. Sir Ronald and Lady Storrs came on Sunday, full of beans and very affable. They called to see us on Saturday afternoon, and stayed for tea. We are invited to Government House, Cyprus one day. The pro-Jerusalem Society is going to be wound up, I think, but Cliff has been offered a new job by the Government. He will be the Town Planning Advisor to the Government in Jerusalem, with permission to advise any other town in Palestine, and also permission to do private work. The contract is for two years.

25th November

Your letter (Elizabeth) was waiting for me when we returned from Syria. We did this time what we wanted to do before, that is drive through Acre to see what it was like. Really, it is very romantic: the fortress looks most imposing when it is near, and inside the town are lots of crusader arches. It all looks very old and far away – like something that has really stood still for a long time – it has quite a character of its own. The mosque is beautiful; we couldn't see inside as it was Friday, but we went into the courtyard, and it is beautiful too. The mosque looks much more like the pictures one sees of the Constantinople mosques, very plain with a dome, flat and simple. The minaret is very tall, thin and graceful, with the top painted bright green. We didn't change our minds about Beirut: it is a nasty place, and not even amusing like Alieh. It was funny to see so many Renaults. We took ours to the garage, had it overhauled and bought some spare parts. Everyone laughed at our poor little Renault, and no-one believes that it went to Syria and back. My driving lessons are few and far between, but I can drive a little, and coming home from Tabgha I drove from the top of the hill above Tiberias to Nazareth, and then right across the Plain of Esdraelon.

Bomberg is in London, and is having an exhibition of paintings at the Leicester Galleries, starting about 8th January, so if you want to see Palestine again, go and see it.

27th December

We are all feeling limp after a riotous Christmas and four strenuous days before it. The strenuous days were caused by Cliff suddenly deciding to build a fireplace in the sitting room. There was a suitable place where there was a blocked-up window, and the wall was very thin. So, one day, Ben Dor arrived with bricks, cement, clay and all the other necessaries, and we started. Bill and I are now expert mortar-mixers, and Cliff and Ben Dor lightning bricklayers and plasterers. We have had made an iron basket of the real old-fashioned kind, which looks lovely full of blazing olive wood and, miracle of miracles, the fire doesn't smoke. It looks wonderfully cheery after the little black stove.

We invited the complete office to tea on Christmas Day, and with the addition of wives, children and brothers and us, the number for tea was 22, so you can imagine we had a riotous time. The tree looked lovely, and everyone set to work to amuse the children, amusing themselves equally at the same time. All came armed with presents for Paul and John, who had so many toys they don't know what to do. Harmat presented Cliff with two large tins of Hungarian paprika. After tea was finished, we lit the tree and the lanterns; everyone had a present and, as many of them had with them musical instruments, we had a jazz band. We had 24 balloons to play with (I think four have survived) and we pulled six dozen crackers. The married guests went home about six, but the odd unattached stayed until eight, and went home down the road in a string singing at the tops of their voices. I believe they carried their gaiety on to friends' houses. Only Mrs Bomberg stayed for dinner, and I can't say we were quiet. Cliff brought the gramophone down, and we danced between courses.

9

1928

Living in a transition from an old to a new age is a theme of a number of events during this year. A smallpox scare occurs, reminding us of the proximity of Palestine to the age-old source of the disease. Although she doesn't mention it in any of the letters, Eunice contracted malaria in Jerusalem. The age of lighting and cooking by oil – albeit paraffin oil – was ending for many with the installation of electricity. More novel and exciting was the wireless, and listening to the news from London. Within a few years it was to be common. And to add to the beginnings of air flights home was a new train service from England to Palestine.

But we are taken back to the primitiveness and desolation of parts of Palestine by the description of a trip along the Jordan valley. Along one stretch of 50 kilometres not a village or a house was seen. 'Why has it that terrible sinister feeling, as if there were something evil in it?' writes Eunice at one point. And at another was the difficulty of finding tracks to take the car along. Perhaps the ancient denudation and erosion of the hills and land between had something to do with Eunice's feelings, that all life and goodness had gone. Then there was the danger of very steep hairpin bends with loose stony surfaces above very steep slopes.

Eunice was pretty discreet about travelling, which was more hair-raising than she suggests. Her sister Elizabeth came out for five weeks in the summer of 1928, and writes home more freely about the road from Jerusalem to Jaffa and its 'terrible hairpin bends'. I remember them vividly, along with buses turning on them and backing to a few inches from the edge.

In addition to these everyday events, others more ominous were stirring in the ever-present tension between Arab and Jew. Trouble was often caused by disputes about the Wailing Wall, the remaining part of the Temple, also sacred to the Muslims because of its association with Mohammed. The Wall, pavement in front and houses beyond were Muslim property, but the Jews had rights to pray at the Wall. On the occasion to which Eunice refers in her letter of the 2nd October, the Jews built a screen across the pavement to divide men from women which, after warning, was removed by the police. The demonstrations went beyond those in Palestine that Eunice describes, becoming worldwide and a matter for debate in Parliament. Unease simmered on before exploding into riots the following year; it was not only incidents that caused trouble. The right wing of the Zionist Movement was demanding a Jewish state, and an Arab Executive was formed to fight the idea. Although Jewish immigration had slowed to a trickle after the peak in 1925, the continued purchase of land and establishment of villages could only increase the tension, even though benefits accrued to the Arabs through the increase in capital investments and agricultural improvement.

The year ends with the news of another baby on the way, this time with no reference to England.

10th January

We had a thrilling experience the other night. A friend of Ben Dor's has a wireless set, and Ben Dor took us to hear it. We heard Moscow, Warsaw, Rome, Constantinople, France, but we could not get England! He had an aerial in the room pointing north towards Europe. Then Cliff turned the aerial facing much more west, towards England and, after a little playing about, got through. We heard quite plainly. The concert was a most absurd play called 'Heart's Desire', full of songs from the 'Maid of the Mountains' and others of about the same period. Ben Dor was in fits, it was all so silly. Cliff knew the songs, and we sang, of course. After that, we heard the news. We heard 'it is now three minutes past ten'. We looked at our watches and they said exactly twelve, then it faded away. If it hadn't, I think Cliff would have stayed up until to hear Big Ben. It seemed so queer to think that people in Gildersome were probably listening to the same things. Cliff wants to buy a wireless more than ever now.

We had a smallpox scare last month. A tramp came in from Damascus and developed smallpox here. There was great excitement, notices all over about vaccination; thousands of people were done in the first few days, including a lot of English. The people from the two inns where the tramp stayed were kept in quarantine until the danger period was over. Anyhow, no-one else had it, and I am very glad none of us were vaccinated, because all chance of catching it has now gone.

24th January

Yesterday Paul said 'I don't want to go to England, there is a lot of cold in England', and John replied at once 'There is a lot of hot in Jericho'; I don't know how he knew.

I must now explain why I was so busy last week. I told you that the architects in Palestine were giving a dance, and that the office had to go as a group. We decided to make an ark and go as Noah and company. As usual, we didn't start until the last minute, with the result that we were working at breathless speed for a week. The men made the ark and the women the costumes. As there were fourteen of us, and only four women with any idea of sewing, it was no easy matter to get the costumes finished on time: Mrs Bomberg, Bill and I sewed like mad. Cliff, as Noah, wore a pair of white trousers, very wide at the bottom and wired to stand out, a rough coat of wolf skin and a very tall hat with a peak, and HMS Ararat on the front. He wore a long white beard and looked very fine. Cornfelt was Ham, a mixture of a South African and a New Brighton black; a Hungarian called Sodmoria was Shem, a Chinese coolie; and Harmat, as baby Jepheth, went as a Greek in white. The rest of us were animals. I was a pink rabbit, and Bill was Felix. We had a kangaroo (complete with pocket and two babies), a snake, butterfly, owl, bat, bear, penguin and monkey. The ark was a very light wooden frame with canvas stretched over the wood, and painted in bright colours with very futuristic designs. It was put up in the hall in the afternoon, and at ten we all climbed through a window and got into the ark without anyone knowing. As it had no bottom, we were able to move it round the room with four people holding it inside and us all walking. It must have looked very funny, as the lifters swayed and rolled the ark in a most realistic manner. We had painted waves on the side which flapped as we moved. At one point in our procession, Noah appeared out of a porthole, and let loose a dove: a real one. Then a rainbow appeared over the top, and we stopped in the middle of the room and all came out singing 'It ain't going to rain any more.' Next, Ham and Shem carried out a small black altar on which we laid the penguin (Mrs Bomberg), beautifully fat, as she was well stuffed with balloons. Noah then stabbed her and she went flat most realistically. Finally we sang an Arabic song and danced round her with some clapping of hands and shouting, then we walked off in procession. Noah and his sons all had stuffed dolls for wives which Mrs Bomberg had made. Someone took such a delight in Mrs Noah's that he bought it for a pound, which Cliff gave towards the proceeds. You can imagine what our house has been like the past week. Fourteen people made themselves absolutely at home here every afternoon for a week. Sewing, being tried on, painting, hammering, having tea - it was all great and I thoroughly enjoyed it. All our rooms lead out of each other, so of course there is no privacy. If I wanted to change, I had to carry my clothes to the bathroom. I am only just getting straight again. In the turmoil, my pen has disappeared.

Tell Mrs Taylor when you write, Mother, that my present servant is a communist. She is a German Jewess, quite a nice girl call Leah. She has lived in Vienna most of her life.

A train service has been started from England to Palestine. What about it? Cliff says Mother (who was afraid of the sea) could fly the channel.

31st January

We have had a very peaceful time since the dance. No excitements or late nights. Cliff has started working on his MA thesis, and hopes this year to really get it through. I spend my two days a week in the office helping him. My communist flourishes, but I fear she will not stay long: she seems too educated to be an ordinary servant. She has numbers of her 'group' visit her, and very wild and ferocious some of them look, especially the Russian element, very Russian and long-haired. Cliff has had another invitation to Cyprus. I think he really must go this time, and I haven't decided whether to go too. I will have to get some new clothes if I do: my wardrobe is not varied enough for Government House.

There are great arguments as to how to get salts from the Dead Sea. The latest idea is a sort of aerial way.

14th February

Lord Plumer is going to live in a biggish house just below us in the Street of the Prophets. They are so tired of being in the cold and bleak convent where they went after the earthquake. Government House will be given back to the Germans. They say we have to return it in a safe condition; the Government says that earthquakes don't count, so I don't know what they will decide in the end. Anyway, the Street of the Prophets will be kept well-mended and well-watered, so we shall benefit.

27th February

We are revelling in about three minutes sunshine. We have had a very exciting week climatically. Firstly, we had an earthquake. Not a very long one, but strong enough to get quite a good sensation. Cliff was on the fourth floor of the Bible House, and felt it very much. I was at home in the sitting room. It's no joke to feel a good solid stone house shaking like a jelly. It was a very small shake, but one imagines it much bigger. There was practically no damage. The atrocious weather continues. I have never known more than four consecutive days of rain before, and we have just had eight. Our garden is like a duck pond, and our cisterns full and running over. It is far too windy to use an umbrella, and we get terribly wet when we go out.

6th March

Mrs Johnson asked me to help with tea at an exhibition, got up by Lady Plumer, of all the arts and crafts of Palestine, very interesting and attractive; the proceeds go to the earthquake fund. We were very glad to have the Bomberg catalogue and cuttings. I am glad that you liked his work. Mrs Bomberg was interested to hear what you said about the red roofs: other people have said the same sort of things. Personally, I like the large city pictures of Sir Ronald's better than the Mount of Olives one, although, of course, the latter is more admired.

9th March

I wish that you could have come with us yesterday. We went a picnic to a most lovely place about an hour's ride from here. It was a very green valley with a stream and flat rocks. On each side were grass fields covered with bright red anemones and pale pink cyclamens. It's a perfect place in spring, and it is such a pity to think that in a few weeks' time all the stream will have dried up and all the flowers will be dead. We picked hundreds of flowers and I have great bowls of them all over the house. Paul and John were in their element, it was so warm they were able to run about naked and paddle in the stream.

On Saturday, we went to a convention of Scottish ministers. Cliff was invited as architect to the Memorial. I had quite a long talk with the Moderator of the United Free Church of Scotland (is that right?). A nice old man with black breeches and lace ruffles.

1st April
Tabgha

We are sitting on a grassy bank at the edge of a little wood of eucalyptus trees. The fields are green, just like England, and full of flowers, some yellow with mustard and big yellow daisies. We had a bathe at seven this morning before breakfast. It was rather cold, but beautifully fresh. There is a hot – more or less – stream flowing into the sea at the bathing place, so after we have been in the sea we can get warm in the pool. It is full of fish. We are the only stable visitors

Father Tepper with Paul and John at Tabgha

84

The Hospice at Tabgha

in the hospice, other people are coming and going all the time. On Friday night, Father Tepper asked us if we would keep the children quiet as the King of Saxonia was sleeping in the next room. We called him the Grand Duke, but I believe he is a prince. Anyway, he was an unpleasant-looking individual with a terrible voice and rather partial to food. He had a collection of equerries and retainers carrying chairs, cameras, binoculars, and even fly switches... The orange trees outside our bedroom are in full bloom and smell wonderful. Paul and John like the lemon trees because they find little lemons underneath which they give to Father Tepper. We have seen fishes, toads, crabs, turtles, kingfishers and storks.

6th April

Last night two newly married people came from Jerusalem with a gramophone, so we took it on the lake and just drifted about in the moonlight. We have great excitement with this boat. It's always anchored at the end of the garden and we often steal it when we are bathing. But the two Bedouin boys who look after it come rushing down to the shore in a state of wild consternation, shouting and waving their arms about. Last night, they got very sarcastic and told us to 'yalla' and go to Tiberias if we wanted to. After that, however, we made peace, and they invited us to a fantasia. One of the young Bedouin in the camp on the hill had just come out of hospital, and they were celebrating. We went up to the black tents and found them all out on the hilltops. The men were dancing their wild dance, a most queer step, round and round with a leader waving a stick, and a little boy playing a pipe in the centre. The rhythm of the dance is wonderful, and they keep absolutely in time, and whatever the leader did the others followed at once marvellously. We were given coffee of course, and very good coffee. The women were all round with their babies: they looked almost wilder than the men, with their black clothes and flowing headdresses, tattooed faces and dyed fingernails.

On Saturday, we all had tea with a countess in a tent! She is a Russian writer and traveller, and has lived with Bedouins in Syria for three months. She is staying here, camping in Father Tepper's little wood. Her husband is an Italian, Count Malmignati; he seems more or less negligible, but is a very amusing and charming person. He only speaks very broken English, but she speaks English perfectly. She showed us a picture of herself in Bedouin dress taken by the *Daily Express*. She came to ask us if we had any English newspapers, so I took her the *Manchester Guardian*, and then she asked us to picnic tea, the children as well. Cliff at the moment is fishing with the Count in the pool. We went to Safad yesterday. We went up 3300 feet in three quarters of an hour, so you can guess how steep the road was. We had a glorious view of Herman with snow on top and the Waters of Merom below.

16th April
We saw an amazing variety of flowers going to Tabgha: cyclamen, anemones, poppies, cornflowers, lovely Spanish iris, great yellow marguerites – whole fields of them – tulips, lupins, huge bright pink things rather like phlox, and lots of other flowers whose names I didn't know... I saw the Holy Fire for the fourth time on Saturday – and I think the last – it gets more orderly each year! But it still thrills me.

22nd April
The Moslems have been making trouble this week. There has been a big missionary conference here and missionaries have taken the opportunity of having public baptisms of converted Moslems. They had a big ceremony at Nablus, and the Moslems were furious and arranged a meeting of protest in the mosque. However, fifty police were sent down and there was no rioting. There was a riot in Gaza; the police had to fire on the crowd, and killed three people. Of course, this has been exaggerated to three hundred. There has been no trouble in Jerusalem, except that the suq was closed for one day, and the day before that, someone threw a stone at the big plate glass curved window of the Bible Society shop. It is a terrible shame, it was semicircular glass especially sent out from England: it cost £50 and was not insured. I suppose a window full of Bibles is too much for some irate Moslems. Lord Plumer refused to lay a foundation stone of the new YMCA because of the trouble. I should think that the Government won't encourage missionaries after this.

2nd May

I never told you about when we took the Renault to Jericho. Earthquake and rain had spoiled the Jericho road, and we had to go by the old Wadi Kelt road. It's terribly steep and curly, and there is one very big hill just at the bottom. We got down all right, but the fun began when we got half way up and the Renault refused to go further. Bill and I had to get out and push. We ran and pushed, and then jumped on the running board, and then off again and more pushing until we finally reached the top. It was exciting.

18th May

The other day, we passed a house and heard music. John, listening, said, 'I want to see that music Mammy'. I said he couldn't because it was inside the house. After thinking a little, John said, 'But mammy, that music has a door'. And Paul said at tea time, 'I wish I had an aeroplane, then I would go and get the moon and play at rolling it in the garden'.

Cliff hopes to have some buildings going up soon. The Scottish Memorial is ready to begin, so are the Soldiers' Home and a Khan for the Opthalmic Hospital and the church at Beirut: they all ought to start this summer. Ben Dor made a lovely model of the Khan, which has gone to England to be put in the Order of St John's Museum.

20th June
A trip to the Jordan Valley
The Hotel Tiberias

This hotel is the noisiest I have ever stayed in. We were awakened at about five this morning and couldn't go to sleep again for shouts, cars, and other noises of all sorts. So, at about half past six, we got up and went down to the lake for a bathe. Cliff is now at a meeting discussing what to do with the town. I must say one cannot see much of the destruction after the earthquake. Tiberias always seems so tumble-down anyway, so I supposed a little more wreckage does not make much difference, but it is sad to see the municipal garden all flattened out and the flowers gone.

For a little peace, we are going to spend tonight in Tabgha. I like Tiberias, in spite of all the bustle, and the lake is so lovely, as ever. Someone was saying last night that HE[4] remarked that there were objections to a speed boat on the lake from religious grounds. The reply was, 'what about a seaplane?'

You will be wondering about the enclosed map: I will explain. It all started with a new motor map of Palestine published by Surveys. It shows several tracks, and as we are so utterly tired of the Nablus/Jenin road – that dreary bit with not a tree on the way – we decided to try the track. When I suggested going down the Wadi Fara and up the Jordan Valley, Cliff said it was much too far, and we would do that when we had a whole day: it was nearly 3.00. However, we somehow missed the joining of the two tracks and suddenly realised we were sailing merrily on a really good road, down the Wadi. So we decided to go on and risk it. The Wadi Fara is really pretty, very green with oleanders and lots of trees by the side of the stream, and the valley is wide and pleasant. In fairly good time we reached Jiflik, and then went along slowly looking for our left-hand turning. But no turning did we see, and we had nearly reached the Jordan. So back we went and looked again and, when Cliff said we must go back to Nablus, my heart sank. However, having got back almost to Jiflik, Cliff noticed a large stone, whitewashed on two sides, the sole indication of a track, which happened to go through the rocks into the hillside. We came out on the other side anyway, and found a track quite clearly marked and easy to follow.

I always wanted to see the whole of the Jordan Valley, but a more desolate place I have never been in. Why has it that terrible sinister feeling, as though there were something evil about it? I think they should make the much-talked-of channel and let in the Mediterranean. It really should be the bottom of the sea, and not high and dry, or low and dry. We had thought it would be a monotonous flat straight track, but not at all. At times, it got almost too exciting. Figure eights weren't in it. We not only went up and down to cross the wadis, but sideways, and the turn and dip always came at the same place, and very suddenly.

Halfway there, we had a puncture and, as we changed the wheel, we saw, with relief, some Bedouin tents on the Jordan banks: because it is 52 kilometres between Jiflik and Beisan, and not a village, or even a house, all the way. We met several herds of camels, one at the bottom of a wadi, and all the camels turned and sped up the sides again, even though we stopped to let them pass. You won't believe it, but Beisan was delightfully cool. It was a quarter to six, and a cool breeze was blowing. We stopped for petrol and water and then went on to Samakh. I looked at the Besian dig, and thought of you sitting palpitating on the top. We got to Tiberias at 7.00, just as dusk was falling. Cliff suggests going home from Haifa by the coast, past Athlit and Caesarea to Lydda and home. Then we shall have done a circular tour all round Palestine.

10th July

It is a good idea to come to Jaffa with Cliff when he has to come down (I am writing in the Municipal Engineer's office). A two hour's ride is a long way to come for one meeting; but if I come too, we have a picnic lunch and two bathes, which makes it worthwhile. It's lovely on the shore where we go, very quiet and peaceful, with occasional strings of camels going past on the sea edge, or a fisherman with a big round net which he flings into the sea when he sees a fish jump.

8th August.

Elizabeth hasn't arrived yet. Cliff and I are thinking of meeting her at Lydda and bringing here up by car… I don't think I told you that the lift has been fixed, at last, in the Bible House. It is the first lift in Jerusalem, and only the second in Palestine. Most of the Arabs, of course, have never seen one before.

17th August

We saw an interesting place yesterday which I had never seen before. It was a piece of the original Via Dolorosa, the old Roman road, two metres below the level of the present road, and part of the arch where Pilot stood with Christ and said 'Behold the Man'. It is all enclosed now in a convent.

Letters from Elizabeth

18th August

We had tea with Miss Nixon yesterday. We were amused by a story she told. Her old Arab servant worked her a tea cosy in greens and blues, and when she handed it over there was one leaf of the pattern embroidered in bright red. Miss Nixon said, 'Oh, what a pity, I could have found you a little blue thread if I had known you were short; but the Arab said, 'Am I God, that I should make everything perfect, and so bring evil on your house?'.

I met a lot of English people at the Broadhursts' party last night. They live in the third most interesting house in Jerusalem (Beit Syriac is, by common consent, the first!). But what an approach! We took a taxi as far as we could, and then dismissed it. There was a new moon, so we had to do the rest by starlight. We seem to have been left on the brink of a rough stony precipice, down which we proceeded to scramble, walking as into an abyss. We could see the lights of Siloam over across the valley. Cliff clung hold of me, because every footstep was a surprise to me. Finally, we saw a light and found ourselves in the entrance hall of a house, and among a gay crowd of people. The house is built into the rock face and the kitchens are caves in the rock! They must be beautifully cool. But from the verandah on the other side of the house we had a magnificent view, even at night.

21st August

This is a funny country. The plumber came this afternoon. He looks just like a student, decked out for an exhibition in shorts and, as Bill said, he probably was a student. I had half an hour's conversation with Leah the cook this afternoon, half in German and half in English. Leah expounded the psychology of Freud and compared it with the later 'individuum psychologie' of Adler, of which I know nothing. Leah was a teacher once, and would like to be a doctor. She is a communist, but dare not acknowledge it. Strange young men and women come in and out of her room in the courtyard; they read and discuss great tomes together, and yesterday, about ten in the evening, we heard a most animated discussion going on. Leah told Eunice this morning that she must leave at once. We can't understand why. Apparently she is quite happy here, likes us all and wants to stay, but must go: the reason is connected with the house somehow. We wonder if she is being watched, as she collects communists together. She is such a nice girl, and a good cook. It is tiresome for Eunice, but 'malaish' says Eunice, and goes singing about the house as usual. Cliff and Eunice get up in the morning singing duets. Bill and Leah sing too and, of course, so do Paul and John.

We saw Cliff and Ben Dor make a model of Barclay's Bank. It was very interesting, and rather an event in the office. Everyone came along to look. The office seems a happy family too, there seem to be such a lot of them. The Bible building is very good indeed. When the bank is up, Post Office Square will be all 'Holliday': and the clock tower is there, and Cliff hopes to build a municipal building. Then there is another 'Holliday' group on the Bethlehem road, with the Scottish Memorial and the Opthalmic Hospital.

26th August

We had a lovely picnic yesterday in Jaffa. While we were camping on the shore, south of Jaffa, we were close upon one of the oldest roads in the world, which leads to Jaffa and down to the seashore, and so south to Gaza. All day long, trains of camels were passing, sometimes in a row strung together. There were Arabs on donkeys, or on horseback, Sudanese on bicycles. I should think it is about 30 miles from Jerusalem to Jaffa as the crow flies, but it is about 56 by road, with terrible hairpin bends. Your hair stands on end as you go up or down. It's like climbing a wall. You pass Arab villages and vineyards in the mountains; also the Jewish settlement, Dilb: on the plain more Arab villages with fields of Indian corn, sesame and orange trees, and then the beautiful town of Ramleh with its crusader tower. Just before Jaffa we passed an RAF encampment: it was most amusing to see a notice on a hut 'Yorkshire Restaurant and Bar'.

28th August

King Feisal and King Fuad came to the re-opening of the Aksa Mosque. We could not see them. because they spent the whole time in the Haram-es-Sherif; but we saw the firework display on Sunday night from our roof.

13th September

I leave here on Saturday morning. The time has simply flown, I can't believe I've been here five weeks. It has been nice… There are two men, connected with the Palestine Police – great friends of Bill and indeed of the whole household – who are returning by the *City of Benares*. We shall probably leave Jerusalem together, and I shall start off the journey with friends, which will be nice. One of them is Irish and one a Yorkshireman (Pringle and Parker). Pringle is a great shot and brings us hare, Jerusalem grouse, chekaw and other game. He shoots stray cats for Eunice, he has shot seventeen in the garden this summer. They – the cats, not Pringle – steal the meat and prowl around generally. Eunice says the poor people round about are most grateful to her and 'the man with the barood' (gun).

This is my last letter; we are picnicking in the Jordan today.

Letters from Eunice

9th September

We got back from our northern trip yesterday. It was very enjoyable, but terribly hot. We left on Tuesday morning at six thirty. It was very cold, driving so early in the morning over the hills, and we didn't really get warm until we reached Sebastieh (Samaria) where we stopped to look at the ruins. There is a big hill on which were once the palace, temple and royal buildings of Herod the Great. It

At Capernaum

Sebastieh

is supposed to have been his country seat and the traditional spot where Salome danced. There are the remains of a rather beautiful crusader church, supposedly built over the tomb of John the Baptist. The remains of the palace and temple are interesting, especially the latter, as it was obviously built on much older remains. There had been a beautiful colonnaded street leading up to the hill, which had a lovely view of the sea: altogether a magnificent site. We left Sebastieh about ten, and passed through Jenin into the Plain of Esdraelon. Then, instead of going the usual way by Nazareth, we branched off to the east, passed a most amusing mud village, and made our way through the Plane of Jezreel to Beisan. This is a 'tel' where American archaeologists are digging, and three people we know are there: Mrs Bomberg, Emmanuel Ben Dor and Kent (an English boy from Cliff's office). It is below sea level and terribly hot, and we were exhausted. After having lunch and seeing the 'tel', we started again up the Jordan Valley: so bare and dry and hot. We passed the Rutenberg scheme (for electricity for Palestine) and so up the lakeside to Tabgha.

17th September
We saw Elizabeth off on Saturday morning, and were very sorry to see her go. Cliff went off yesterday morning at six to Beirut with Ben Dor and Cornfelt in the new Fiat. They have gone to see the new church, which will be started quite soon now.

2nd October
We had a Jewish row this past week. On Tuesday was a big fast day for the Jews, when they repent all their sins. For the occasion, they built a temporary wall

across the road leading to the Wailing Wall. But as the road happened to be a right of way, the Moslems went to the Governor and objected. The police were sent, and gave the Jews three hours to take the wall down. At the end of that time they had done nothing, so the police broke it down themselves. There was a terrible row. On Thursday there were demonstrations in every town: all shops shut et cetera, and unfortunately we were coming back from Jaffa, and reached Jerusalem at the time they all came out of their meeting. Imagine us – in the car – suddenly finding ourselves in the middle of a crowd of several thousand irate Jews. Fortunately, Cliff has so many friends of various kinds that we soon saw several people he knew, who all came round and explained and told us not to worry (not that we were frightened, it was rather exciting). There were yells of 'down with Duff' (the police officer) and 'down with Keith Roach' (the District Commissioner) all round us. They cut the telephone wires and tried to rush a police station: it failed, of course. Finally, the head of the Zionist Commission came and harangued the crowd in Hebrew. They sang their National Anthem, and then got the head of the commission on their shoulders and took him off down the Jaffa Road. At this point we were able to go home. We hear that on Saturday, the Supreme Moslem Council summoned the Moslems from all the villages by telling them that the Jews wanted to take the mosque back again. They wanted to have a procession, but the police put their feet down.

11th October

Cliff is busy putting the final touches to the Scottish Memorial drawings. They should begin to build now. The latest item of interest is that our road is being widened and tarred, and having pavements on each side. This will be a great improvement, as we shall have less dust. Mrs Garstang rang up yesterday to ask if she and the Professor could come to lunch, so I had to assemble a meal in a hurry (soup, crab mayonnaise, sweetbreads and fried potatoes, cheese and biscuits, fruit and coffee). We were very glad to see them again. The Department of Antiquities has been very dull since they left. Mrs G. is as talkative as ever, and gave us lots of Liverpool news.

We went a picnic to Jaffa: the Fiat goes beautifully! Mrs Keith Roach is coming round this afternoon to persuade me to sell poppies to the British people around here. She will probably succeed, as I have no serious reason for refusing. Poppy selling has never been done here before. We have workmen all along the road now, digging us up. The wall that belonged to Sir Ronald Storrs' garden is being moved back to make the road wider, and Cliff has been busy with Mr Park (Municipal Engineer) arranging things so that the trees don't have to be cut down. The workmen sing as they work. They make a big noise, and periodically, also, we have a barood, which is a blasting of rock. We hear the warning cry 'barood, barood'.

30th October

Cliff had a free morning on Saturday, so we went down to Jericho and took lunch. We encamped by a stream in the middle of the orange groves. Paul and John bathed. We bought oranges and sweet lemons, picking them ourselves from the trees. Going back to the car, we met Mrs Garstang, who was sitting by a pool washing pieces of pottery. Her husband was digging on the site of old Jericho. He is trying to find the walls which fell down, and so establish the actual date of the coming of the Children of Israel.

4th November

Now, I have some very important news: I am going to have another baby. We are very pleased. Paul will be six-and-a-half and John four-and-a-half, and it will be a summer baby, for a change.

16th November
The German Hospice, Haifa

We had a very good run here on Thursday. We didn't start until ten, and then, just outside Jerusalem, we passed the RAF landing ground and saw two aeroplanes, so of course Paul and John wanted to see them. So we didn't get to Nablus until lunch time, and arrived in Haifa just in time for tea. We are staying in the Hospice in the town this time, as it is rather cold on Carmel. We are only five minutes walk from the shore, so very near the railway line (much to John's joy) and there is a beautiful garden here for the children to play in.

7th December

The High Commissioner (Sir John Chancellor) arrived yesterday. There was a reception at Jaffa Gate. He is an imposing-looking man and his uniform is marvellous. Lady Chancellor looked very nice.

14th December

I was very successful with my stall, which looked most attractive. I made £22 10/-. Khoury, the best shop here, gave me, after much persuasion, a big baby doll, which a friend dressed beautifully, and Cliff and Bill raffled it. They made £5 10/-. The whole bazaar made £400. Lady Chancellor opened it and made a nice friendly speech.

You have probably heard from Yorkshire that Grandpa is dead. I expect there will be a big migration from Gildersome now.

20th December
Tiberias

Cliff is here on duty, so I am here too. We came yesterday in the Fiat. We ran into rain at Nablus, and also into mud! After lunch, Cliff had a town planning meeting, and then we walked to the hot baths, which is quite a long way. We heard running water through a hole near the baths, so we put our fingers in, and it was nearly boiling. Tomorrow we set off for Haifa. Cliff has to see a few people there, and also we've found a German shop full of lovely toys, so will be getting our Christmas things here.

10

1929

The year began with thoughts about moving house, because of building nearby, and with the anticipation of a third child and the prospect of Paul going to school, which would be in another part of Jerusalem. But perhaps the location of the house also influenced the family, for it was near the old city and, at the beginning of the major riots of August, Eunice writes of the Jews in hundreds rushing down the Street of the Prophets, in which the house stood.

These were the most serious riots since the Mandate had been established. Although they were triggered by an incident at the Wailing Wall, there had been a few killings the previous week and a heightening of tension, caused by the Zionist Congress aiming to widen activities in Palestine. In the eventual riots, over 250 people were killed and nearly 600 wounded. Neither were the riots and killing all in Jerusalem, but took place in many towns throughout the country. The Palestine Police Force had been reduced to a level at which it was incapable of controlling riots: troops had to be brought in from Egypt, and British civilians were called up to a special force. Cliff was included in this, no doubt adding spice to the children's life with uniforms and guns, but it must have been quite frightening for Eunice. Cliff was in Jaffa at the start, and had an adventurous homecoming, being stopped in turn by Arab and Jewish mobs. His Arab office boy, Jameel, got them through the first mob and some recognition of Cliff by Jews through the second. Things simmered on through September and, as Eunice puts it, 'there is a little quiet murder every day.'

A commission of MPs came out from England in October, and sat until December, reporting to Parliament in March. Amongst various things, in which the issues of land and immigration were highlighted, they recommended that the Government should issue a clear statement of policy, and this they did, emphasising an obligation to the Arabs in the face of growing Jewish nationalism.

There were to be no more serious riots until 1936, by which time the family had returned to England.

1st January

What do you think: Paul is learning eurhythmics? Mrs Yellin (the cellist and Mr Bentwich's sister) has two little girls, and has been trying to get up a class for some time and now one has been formed by a Jewish girl who studied under Calcrose. There are nine little children, all Jewish except Paul, and she teaches in Hebrew! I didn't know if Paul would be able to do it, not understanding a word of the instructions, but he had the first lesson today and managed so well, by just watching the others and listening to the music, that I will let him go on. He loved it and was quite exhilarated afterwards. The instructress (with an unpronounceable name) said he had a very good ear. He has to go next time in a little black bathing costume.

14th January

Did I ever tell you that we shall probably leave this house at Muharram (the movable feast when people move, this year in June). The Syriacs are continuing their row of shops right in front of our bedroom and nursery windows, and there is sure to be a horrid collection of rubbish and flies at the back of the shops, and that will mean that we have to keep the windows at that side shut all the time. This is going to lead to all sorts of new plans for the next year. First, we have decided that Paul should go to school. Mr Dawson and Miss Miller have started a school in the Greek Colony. If Paul goes, we must live in the Greek Colony, a thing I always said I'd never do. Then Bill will go in the autumn, so if I send Paul to school, and look after John until he can go, I can get some Arab or German girl to help with the babe. Cliff thinks we need a change, and I believe he is right.

5th February

Mr Pearcy, who is looking after the building of the Scottish Memorial, rang on Monday to say that, in digging for foundations, they had opened up a tomb containing three skeletons. I thought it was rather exciting, but he's very annoyed, for it may hold up the work for a month for more. Antiquities Department have to be notified and examine the tomb.

Cliff has gone to Tel Aviv to a football match. It is an important one for the cup, and this year Cliff is on the committee. He has taken in the Fiat a varied collection of football enthusiasts.

19th March

Cliff went down to the Bristol Garden one night and was greeted with, 'there are some Yorkshire people over there: you had better go and talk to them'. So he went to find that the three girls were Waddiloves, cousins of Dorothy (*Cliff's brother Harry's wife*), and the boy a friend of George Blackwell (*a relative of*

Eunice)! They were on their way to Cairo, and the boat had stopped at Haifa. All the girls knew about Cliff was that Harry had a very quiet brother who was always reading books!

Easter Monday was a lively day. Bill went off for the day with Parker. Sophie came to play with Paul and John, and Cliff and I took Mr and Mrs Everiss to Jericho and the Jordan. It was nicely hot. We gathered armfuls of lovely yellow marguerites, and the scent of the orange blossom was wonderful. It was too muddy to have lunch on the banks of the Jordan, so we had to go further off under the tamerisk trees. I went prospecting for a dry spot, and suddenly found myself up to the knees in thick mud. Mr Everiss had to scrape it off with a penknife.

8th April

I forgot to tell you in my last letter that we saw the *Graf Zeppelin*. It is a monstrous thing. I'd love to have seen it in the daytime, but it came over about eight in the evening. Fortunately, the moon was up and we could see it quite well. It's terrific, so big. Paul and John had been so anxious to see it that when Ben Dor rang at seven to say it had just left Tel Aviv, they wouldn't go to sleep. So, when we sighted it, we wrapped them up in their eiderdowns and brought them out on the roof to see. It reminded me of the time Father got me out of bed and hung me out of the bedroom window to see Haley's comet. The Zeppelin circled over Jerusalem twice and then went over towards the Dead Sea. Once it went right over our house and we had a splendid view.

23rd April
To Elizabeth

Pringle came round on Sunday evening with Parker. He was full of enquiries about you, and how he had enjoyed the trip on the boat and his visit to Royal Holloway College. Oh, and Ali has been and asked after you. Poor man, he gets blinder and blinder. He says he is 85 years old. I went to the doctor yesterday: he says he can't feel two babies, so don't get excited. Bill is as bad as you are: she calls them 'Lois and Louis'.

29th April

We had a nice Passover dinner at Shiffman's. It was quite small and quiet, but with all the ceremonials. Cliff was given a little black velvet cap to wear. I wore my Chinese coat, which was much admired by everyone. The Everisses came on Saturday, and we took out tea to Ain Kareem, which is a lovely village, very green and fertile (the home and birthplace of John the Baptist). We found heaps of flowers and some real honeysuckle. John was in his element: I think he would pick flowers indefinitely; he just loves flowers. We saw a very black Abyssinian in the fields, so we told John to go and speak to him. John went up and shook hands and said 'Said, kif halik', which means 'Good day, how do you do'. He is very fond of the black porter who brings our bread. Perhaps it is because they have such lovely smiles. Paul has been very happy this week helping Cliff decarbonise the car. He simply revels in passing tools and unscrewing and greasing joints et cetera. He greeted me with a large smile and remarked 'Oh mammy, I do love to be sticky'. All the roads are partially up in Jerusalem, as we are having electric cables put down.

1st June
I heard a very nice story the other day. The Orthodox Jew will not eat sole because it is only half a fish, and therefore not Kosher. When the Red Sea divided for the Children of Israel, a sole got in the way and was cut in half, hence its flatness. Each half of the sole grew another eye, but it is still only half a fish. Perhaps this is why the Arabic name is 'Samak Musa' which means Moses's fish.

8th June
Cliff went off at 5.00 this morning to Beirut: he took the Parks for company. The church is nearly finished: they hope to have the consecration at the end of the month.

14th June
Did I tell you that the High Commissioner was going to Cliff's office to see his work? He went on Wednesday, and stayed for an hour, looking at plans and drawings. Cliff found him very nice and interested. Apart from this, HE has a new car with a crown on and a chauffeur, who is a blue-eyed yellow-haired English boy who goes by the nickname of Mabel.

21st June
I've enquired about the public houses in Palestine! There may have been only four licensed houses before the war, but there were plenty of places where people could get arak and other drinks. I expect a little bakshish did away with the need for a licence! Arak is the chief strong drink here: it is a spirit which tastes like aniseed and is made locally from grapes. It goes milky when water is added to it. The strict Moslems, who are teetotal, complain that the English have brought drink into the country. True, I don't suppose they had whisky before. Anyway, one very rarely sees a drunken man here.

24th June
Telegram
Eight pound Timothy arrived at 1.00am. All well.

28th June

I've given up! I'm evidently incapable of producing daughters. Anyway, nobody could possibly regret Timothy because he is so beautiful. You will see I am not at the Government Hospital. Dr MacQueen rang up about three weeks ago to say that Mrs Pope, who had just had a baby, was ill with erysiplis and, as it was infectious, I decided to come here (Dr Danziger's private hospital). We are so glad that I did, as Mrs Pope got blood poisoning and other things, and died on Saturday. It was all very sad. This is a very nice place. Dr Danziger and his wife run it, and there is one Danish Christian Sister – Sister Jenny, a charming and kind person – who looks after me. Everything is very clean and white, very orderly and methodical. Paul and John don't seem to mind having a brother, though Paul's remark on hearing it was a boy was 'Oh, now we can't use the pink side of the eiderdown!'

1st August
From Tan Tur, Bethlehem

We are staying here for a fortnight. Tan Tur is an Italian convent, a lovely place high on the hills just half way between Jerusalem and Bethlehem. It is very quiet and peaceful, and beautifully fresh and cool. There is a lovely garden for the children, and a small farm with cows, chickens, sheep and lots of white rabbits with pink eyes. Timothy lies about and gets fatter and browner. The sisters overwhelm us with kindness, and they have given us a private room, because they think it is better for the children. There is an over-abundance of fresh milk to drink, and hot water for washing (quite an item for us). There are only four sisters besides the Mother Superior. How they run this great place I can't imagine: they must work terribly hard. The two we see most are Sister Mathilde and Sister Madelaine. There are very long verandahs and balconies, and Paul and John spend their time simply racing up and down.

Cliff has joined the sports club, and taken up tennis and cricket. He suddenly decided he wasn't getting enough exercise, and it has certainly done him good.

8th August

Paul and John have been busy today. They have been picking almonds in the fields with four little Arab children who live here. Now all six of them are sitting in a room round an enormous heap of almonds, taking the nuts out of their green outer shells and putting them in a big basket. Afterwards, all the nuts are spread on the roof to dry.

Last night, we went into Jerusalem after dinner, and I saw the Scottish Memorial for the first time for about three months. It is up to the first floor and the church is begun. It looked awfully nice, as far as I could see by starlight. The church Cliff built in Beirut is to be consecrated at the beginning of November, and we are thinking of going up and having Timothy christened there. I think it would be nice to have him christened in Daddy's first church!

29th August

I have so much to say, I don't know where to begin. We knew there was going to be a row. For a week there had been odd incidents, Jews aggravating Arabs, and Arabs stabbing Jews. One of the stabbed Jews had a public funeral, with a demonstration down the Jaffa Road and speeches in Hebrew, to the effect that 'if the Government won't protect us, we will protect ourselves'. They little knew what they were in for. The police had to stop the procession, because they wanted to go by the Jaffa Gate, and then there would have been a row. Anyway, on Thursday, anybody with a Moslem servant knew something was going to happen. Mahmoud came in, all agog with excitement and brandishing a very aggressive-looking knife. I don't know what they were told in the mosque on Friday, but they all came out determined to kill Jews. Of course all the Moslems believe that the Jews want the Temple area: it's all this wretched Wailing Wall. The new Jews will make trouble. The last thing they did was to take their national flag and put it up on the Wailing Wall. It is rumoured that the Grand Mufti told the villagers that the British would not interfere! The first thing we heard was at

The Wailing Wall

12.30 on Friday. Shouting in Mea Shearim, followed by a shooting, a car-load of police going down the road, then the Jews: there were hundreds of them all with sticks, stones, pieces of iron, even bottles, anything to hit with. They all went rushing down the Street of the Prophets. Next, we saw the ambulance, then all afternoon we watched police cars, an armoured car, Jews, wounded people being brought to the Hadassah Hospital. Cliff had gone to Jaffa, and was told half way home not to come on any further. However, he decided to risk it. Fortunately he had Jameel with him: first they were stopped by a mob of Arabs, but as Jameel told them Cliff was English, they let him go. Next, they were stopped by a mob of Jews, but fortunately again, he knew some of them personally, so he was saved and got home none the worse.

Army and police at the Damascus Gate during the 1929 riots

Army and police at Bethlehem during the 1929 riots

5th September

Well, it's nearly 4.00 and nothing, as yet, has happened this Friday. The Arabs would be rather fools to try. At twelve, the time they come out of the mosque, there were fifteen aeroplanes circling over the City, three, in particular, flying low and looping the loop over the Haram area. Bill, who is my shopper, says there are machine guns and armoured cars all round the Jaffa Gate, and I expect the Damascus Gate is the same. We've got a lot of army up from Egypt and the Sudan. The Russian Building is full of soldiers, and closed to the public. We went through this morning when John went to the hospital to have his stitch out. Seeing the armoured (almond) cars at close quarters was ample compensation for a cut in the head and a stitch. The boys were thrilled when Cliff joined the army of Specials and came home in khaki with a revolver. He had an exciting job on Sunday. It was to go with two other cars and hold up Arabs on the Nablus road and search them. It did not turn out to be as thrilling as they expected: they only got sticks, penknives and a few daggers. One man offered them his watch! Still, guns have been smuggled in, and several houses found to be full of ammunition: Arabs', of course. The most dreadful affair is the shooting and looting in the Jewish Colonies. One man who has been developing a farm for forty years, and employed Arabs all the time, has been left with nothing: literally nothing but his clothes. Very fortunately Delb has been saved: they got the soldiers there in time. The trouble is that the Arabs are armed and the Jews are not. The Hebron affair is too awful to write about. You know the Hebron Arabs are particularly wild and fierce, and they simply massacred the Jews: and they are not European Jews, but the old religious ones who have lived there for centuries, unharmed. We have got sixty Hebron men in prison. You know Talpioth? The Jews were taken out and brought to the city for protection, but whilst they were here, the Arabs looted the place and smashed several houses to bits. One is burnt to the ground, and what hasn't been carried off has been smashed.

Do you remember reading about the Beni Sakhr tribe in Lawrence's book? The chief of the tribe was met on the Jericho road the other day by someone who recognised him. He said he was paying a visit to the Mufti, and that he came every year! He was told he would be safer in the hands of the Government and is now in prison. We heard the Wahabies were marching on Amman, but that has stopped. I think the Arabs would like a jolly old war.

It is a pity that the Jews are so aggressive about their rights; they simply ask for trouble, but they certainly didn't expect this upheaval. They will have lost terribly. Cliff saw, in one colony, a stable full of cows, eighteen all burnt, and they cost £100 each. Very fortunately the army came just in time to save Tel Aviv. The soldiers who were sent to Jaffa marched from the station into an Arab mob, who were just about to march to Tel Aviv. They killed forty Arabs. We hear a lot of firing in the hills at night, but I think we're quiet now in the city. Cliff has been back at the office for two days. Bill goes to Tulipman's and the post every day, but I haven't been out for a week, except once in a car with a police escort. Talking of Lawrence, there is a rumour amongst the Jews that he organised all this! It is marvellous what the Jews will believe… I expect next week everything will be quite normal.

September

I think all the trouble is over now. Everything is going on as usual, but I expect we will have soldiers here for some time. We didn't suffer at all from lack of food. We thought we might, so the second day Cliff went down in the car to one English grocer who was open, and bought a great supply of tinned stuff, several loaves, and about ten tins of milk. (Our milk lady did not turn up for a week.) So we had plenty to eat and the shops gradually opened after Sunday. Now all is normal again.

I must say, it was rather exciting whilst it lasted, and I certainly felt a little nervous (especially when Cliff was 'specialling' at night and there were snipers about). However, nervousness didn't seem to affect Timothy, although I thought it might. Of course Bill was thrilled, she wanted to go out and fight all the time. We still have a curfew, and no-one is allowed out after six. Some Government officials are still being Specials and patrolling the streets at night. The boys in the office are all right. Ben Dor spent the first few days running about in the Renault, working for the hospitals. They opened a baby hospital for the poor little children from Hebron, and he came and took my old pram. We had a shock one night when someone rang up to say that Chaikin had been shot. Cliff went down to his house at once, only to find it was a rumour. We felt it might be true, as it was the day the English Jews had been disarmed. They were allowed to be Specials at first, but that was altered as the Arabs went about saying the English were arming Jews against them. I've just been to see Bill; the operation was rather sudden. She had had pains in the region of the appendix, and after a few days they got worse, so I said she had better have it out. Everything was quite successful, and she is getting on splendidly. I've got a funny old thing to help me – a sort of missionary – who was doing welfare work in Hebron; but she found it all too much of a shock to live there any more. She is quite nice, more help with Timothy than with Paul and John, and a great assistance with sewing.

12th September

Cliff's fed up with Palestine – what with one thing and another – the bank settlement seems to have been shelved indefinitely now and other jobs aren't hurrying, except the ones actually going up. He says we're not coming home until we come for good and all. I don't know when that will be! I shan't until about a week before.

27th September

It is Friday again, and there are rumours of another row, but it's a quarter past one, and nothing has happened yet, so perhaps nothing will. There are soldiers at each gate of the city searching Arabs for arms, but not thoroughly, I fear, because Mohammed has just told me, with great glee, how Mahmoud got in with a dagger on the inside of his stocking and the soldiers only felt his outside. We have had no big riots since the first few days, but there is a little quiet murder nearly every day. An Arab kills a Jew, then a Jew goes off and kills an Arab. It's a case of reprisals all the time. The Jews are making themselves very unpopular by being so aggressively 'injured'. I was talking to an Arab the other day (one who has been educated in England and America) and he was saying that seven hundred years ago the Moslems granted the Jews the privilege of praying at the Wall they have wailed at ever since. But now the new Jews (who are not religious at all, and never wail at all) do silly things: first they put up shelves for the prayer books, then seats, then a barrier across, then the flag on the Wall. Naturally, the Arabs do not think that they will stop at that, and when the mosque is threatened, all the fellaheen are up in arms, and you can't blame them. That is the lever the Mufti uses now. Fakhri Effendi, the Mayor's cousin, told Cliff they were having meetings every night in his house, and that rioting and killing will never stop until the Balfour Declaration is stopped. The Arabs have started an English edition of their newspaper 'Falestine'. It is rather interesting: I'm sending a copy home, together with a few Jewish newspapers, so you can read what each side says. The Jews are very bitter and down on us. They say the British police stood and watched Jews being killed and did nothing. Pringle tells us he actually watched Jews being murdered by the Damascus Gate, but they were six policemen against several hundred Arabs. We hadn't enough police in the country, of course, but the ones we did have were splendid. Cliff kept meeting Pringle and Parker, all dirty and muddy and unshaven. When the soldiers came, it didn't relieve them very much because they didn't know the country or the Arabs; in fact they never seem to have done any serious soldiering before. They were all very small, fair, blue-eyed and young. The Arabs are all saying it is a shame to send out such little boys, they ought to be at home with their mothers! Anyway, we now have two hundred new police, and they are all over six feet.

Cliff has sacked all his staff! Cornfelt, Harmat, Ben Dor, all gone. They were all getting very slack, and as there isn't much work to be done now, and the bank keeps being delayed, he thought it was a good opportunity to send them off, and start afresh later if necessary. We all hope to go to Tabgha in October. I am enclosing a photo of the Specials being reviewed by HE. Cliff is the little one in the front row near HE. They are all demobbed now. I can't say I like Cliff being out, especially when the car had been shot at in Talpioth. By the way, this is the kind of things the Jew do. Some Specials were escorting bus-loads of Jews from

Talpioth when they were evacuating. After a lot of fuss, they would get a bus-full and say off, and then suddenly a Jew would remember something he'd forgotten, and another and another. At last the police would get fed up (they were being sniped at all the time) and use a little strong language. Then we would read in the paper the next day that the Jews were treated impertinently and cursed by the British police.

4th October
The two hundred new police have arrived: we know them by their white knees! We are all quiet at the moment, though odd Jews keep being murdered. The Mayor (an Arab) said to Cliff, 'All you English just go down to Kantara for 48 hours, and then you can all come back and we'll live happily together'. Poor Jews.

11th October
Bill is quite well again, and able to do her normal work, but I have only one small boy in the kitchen at the moment. These small boys do get through a surprising amount of work, and very quickly. There is an emergency first aid room in the Russian Compound where all the soldiers are camped. Coming through, one evening, Paul fell quite near and hurt his knee. Bill was trying to tie it up with Paul's very small handkerchief when a soldier came out and offered first aid. Paul was so excited – with his large bandage – he ran all the way home to tell us.

Cliff has a permit to be out after nine. One night we were stopped by a sentry who said, 'Halt' and pointed his bayonet at us: it was most exciting. When he looked at us all carefully he said, 'Pass friend, all's well'. We are quite peaceful now; no more murders. We hear the Hebron people are asking the surviving Jews to come back. Anyway, the police are being very careful until the Day of Atonement is over.

16th October
We had the Day of Atonement on Monday, when the Jews fast all day and confess their sins of the past year. Of course they flock to the Wailing Wall on these occasions. There is a small mosque by the Wailing Wall, so the High Commissioner ordered it to be locked for the day. The Arabs were furious at the insult of a Christian closing a mosque (it was a rather tactless thing to do). So they shut their shops by way of protest. About twenty or thirty Arabs went up to the office and found Jameel (the office boy) and a little Arab student working, and told them to stop at once. We hear the crowd overturned several cars which were being driven by Arabs who refused to stop work. I don't know what will be the end of all this. Both Arabs and Jews think we are favouring the opposite party.

Everything seems to have quietened down here. There are big crowds round the Law Courts all day, where they are trying some of the cases. They don't seem to be able to do much with the Hebron people because, although people know lots of the murderers, they have no definite proof.

Cliff is enjoying having a quite empty (almost) office, and getting a lot of work done in consequence. The Scottish Memorial is up to the roof, and looking very nice; so is the Khan. Ben Dor has got a little office on his own, and several jobs as clerk of works. Harmat is looking for a job: if he doesn't get one, he is going back to Budapest. Cornfelt is working on the new YMCA.

29th October
At last we are in Tabgha. It is lovely to be here again… it's over a year since we had a holiday. Everything is just the same; the oranges just beginning to turn yellow, and the old gazelle paces up and down. Everything seems very peaceful, Father Tepper and his Bedouins still live happily together. I expect there will be Arab demonstrations on Saturday, which is 'Balfour Day'.

13th November
We arrived home last night, having had a safe journey, though we did have two punctures, one before and one just after Jenin. We thought of coming back via the Jordan Valley and Beisan, but decided it might take too long. I was glad we didn't, as it was quite hot enough along the usual road. The antelope (which we always called a gazelle) was finally killed this morning. We were very careful to get the children out of the way, but John said, quite calmly, 'Are we having him for lunch?' The same afternoon, two Bedouins brought in a small wild pig for Father Tepper to buy.

15th November
Bill is going home in January. It is her own decision, but I am rather glad. She is no use at all with Timothy. It's very queer, but if ever I leave him with her, he practically always cries all the time, then she gets all worked up and nervous, and he is such a good baby really. Also, I am going to send Paul to school in January. He wants to go with Sheila, and he really needs the companionship of older children.

Cliff is busy, and beginning to take an interest in the bank now that the contract is signed. Everybody admires the Scottish Memorial. It is to be opened at Easter, when a lot of important Scottish people are coming out, and when Timothy is to be christened.

When we were in Tabgha, Cliff took Paul and John out in the car, and they called on Lord Melchett's house, which he has had built on the lakeside. Cliff had to see Mr Weizman, who is usually there, but he was out, so the housekeeper showed them over the house. The house is built in the middle of a lot of orange and banana plantations, and near the site of Magdela, where Mary Magdelene used to live. All is quiet here now. We await the report of the Commission, though I don't see what they can do, for I don't think either Arabs or Jews will ever be satisfied.

I have been having great fun with the Christmas pudding. Mrs Beeton said boil four hours, so I boiled it four hours, and it came out a miserable pasty-faced thing. I didn't know what to do, so Cliff suggested boiling it some more. After another three hours, it was just getting a really good brown complexion on the outside, so I boiled it another three hours, and now it looks really like a pudding!

20th December

Paul and John are very excited about their two big parties, because Father Christmas will be there.

I suppose in your lecture on dress you will concentrate on headgear? Do you remember the little bit in Chesterton's New Jerusalem about the tarbush, which is a hat which cannot be taken off to a Lady? Don't forget: the tall Bethlehem hat is only for married women, unmarried wear a veil; the Jews always wear their hats in church; Moslem women often unveil before Englishmen, but never before Arabs; fellaheen shoes are very broad, like camel's feet. There is now a new industry in the suq for making shoes with soles made from old car tyres.

11

1930

This was an eventful year for the family. Paul started school, they moved home from Jerusalem to Bethlehem, went on an adventurous visit to Petra, had Cliff's father and mother out from England: Cliff's father died on the way home.

The school was a new one, run by a Miss Miller and catering for a number of nationalities living in and near the Greek Colony. The colony was on the south side of Jerusalem, and at one time Eunice assumed that they would find a house there. In the event, a home, Beit Nassar, was found near Bethlehem. This was just north of Rachel's tomb, and stood in four acres of its own small fields, which came with the house and were treated by the children as a garden. The house itself was large, and is best appreciated from the photograph. Opposite the house were more fields in which we used to roam, finding mosaics and mother of pearl, which was much worked for the tourist industry in Bethlehem. It was a fairly lonely spot, and I was afraid to go out after dark following an incident in which a man was knocked down by a lorry near our front gates, his brother chasing the driver into our house cellar, brandishing a knife. The potential murderer was locked in the cellar by our Arab help, Jameel.

Before the move, Eunice had again written about returning home, saying that they would not take any leave this year, but would return in May 1931. Again they did not.

In March, Professor Abercrombie arrived from England. He had been at Liverpool University when Cliff and Eunice were there, and was later to prepare the Greater London Plan. For now, he had come out to work with Cliff on the Haifa Bay Development Scheme. He was later to work with Cliff from their office in London, and on the new university in Kandy, Ceylon. This year, Cliff and Eunice went to Petra with Prof. Abercrombie and an architect friend, Thomas Concannon. The trip to Petra is described at some length, and was a major adventure in those days, risky both on the journey and at Petra itself, where an armed guard sat at the entrance to the caves where they slept.

In May, Cliff's father and mother arrived and stayed at Beit Nassar. The trip seems to have been enjoyed, but disastrous at the end, for Mr Holliday died in Port Said on the way home. Mrs Holliday was met at Marseilles by Cliff's brother Harry, who took her home.

The final news of the year was the opening of the Scottish Memorial Church in November. The photograph shows it at the time of completion. Now the site is well covered by trees and built on. Then, it stood very much on its own bare hillside, a conspicuous building. A good deal of study has been done lately on the work of architects during the British Mandate. Much was built in the modern international style, but some took more notice of traditions in Palestine, and this church was one. In his autobiography, *Orientations*[3], Sir Ronald Storrs writes that 'Holliday... by his private architectural practice, was providing a corrective to the Central European proclivities of some of his colleagues'. Certainly, Cliff was very sensitive to the conflicting demands of history as they manifested themselves in Jerusalem.

21st January
Paul began school last week. I thought I told you that Mr Dawson (the funny man) had started with a Miss Miller in the Greek Colony. Last term, Mr Dawson left, and Miss Miller is keeping on the school by herself. It is a jolly little school, of course rather far away, and at the moment, Cliff takes Paul in the car and Bill calls for him in the bus at twelve. By reports I have heard, the children don't learn very much, but I think I prefer that to learning too much, and anyway what I want more for Paul is the companionship of boys of his own age. He is getting a little bossy with John. Cliff has suggested taking the boys at the school for football, and Miss Miller is delighted. I didn't consider the kindergarten at the High School because I don't like the mistresses very much, and Cliff definitely objects to them. Paul enjoys school enormously, and John is a marvel at keeping himself occupied all alone. He has various balls in different parts of the house and garden, and goes from one to another all the time.

15th February
We have decided not to come home on leave this year, but to stay here until a year in May, and then come home for good. The bank will be finished then, and Cliff will renew his contract with the Government until then. He can't leave until the bank is finished. I am sorry you won't see Timothy sooner, but it can't be helped. You will see him when he is two, a nice age. We shall move into a new house this May, and will have a year in the Greek Colony amongst the 'Inglesi'. It will be quite a change from living here.

21st February
We have just come from the station after seeing Bill off. She was sorry to go, I think. There were lots of people to see her off besides us: Pringle, Parker, Elise

Abramson and her mother, Mr Maxwell (Minister of Christ Church) and Ben Dor. I am trying a young girl for Timothy: she has had some experience of nursing at the Government Hospital and seems very careful and clean about bottles et cetera. I am waiting to see her reference before I decide whether to keep her. She is English.

Paul and John are out with Cliff going round the buildings. They start off at the Holy Sepulchre. I think I told you that Cliff is redecorating Calvary Chapel. He was working there all last Saturday morning, when he discovered that a black panel in the vault of the ceiling is an old mosaic, in a very good state of preservation, but so covered with the dirt of centuries, that no-one knew it was there. It is a figure of Christ, probably about a thousand years old. Cliff spent the whole morning washing it with soda solution and ammonia. The walls of the chapel are to be panelled with marble, and a mosaic design for the vaulting has been sent from Italy. It is very rare for the Catholics to let a Protestant do any work of this kind for them.

We are wondering whether to go and live in Bethlehem for a year. We are going house-hunting this weekend. It isn't going to be easy to find a house big enough, to rent, and with a garden. Cliff is very bucked just now because we are expecting Professor Abercrombie out at the beginning of April. He is to advise on the Haifa Bay Development Scheme. He will be out a month, and we are hoping he will spend part of the time with us. It will be very nice to have him.

Bethlehem market

22nd March

We are very thrilled, we've got a lovely house in Bethlehem. Not really in Bethlehem, but just at the beginning, near Rachel's tomb. Twelve minutes in the car from Jerusalem. It's a very nice house, with big verandahs overlooking hills on both sides and an enormous garden consisting of several fields of all kinds of trees: apricot, apple, almond, olive, fig, pomegranate, mulberry and a small vineyard. Doesn't it sound lovely? It's all so fresh and open, it will be lovely for the children, and so quiet that Cliff will have time to study and perhaps take his degree. It is near Tan Tur, the Convent we stayed at last summer. What about coming to see it?

Beit Nassar, near Bethlehem

Outside the house: Eunice (back), Paul, John, Timothy,
Ellie and a friend

From Tan Tur

We have left Beit Syriac for good an' all. You see, Cliff had to go to Haifa with
Professor Abercrombie, and I didn't particularly want to be left with the children
in our house for the Nebi Musa procession this weekend, in case there was any
trouble. I don't think there will be, in fact I hear the Arabs are laughing at us for
making so many preparations in the way of army, guns, police et cetera. Still, I
wasn't running any risks, so we came here yesterday and we shall move from there
straight into the new house, which is about five minutes walk away. I had to

Tan Tur Hospice

empty the furniture from one half of the house into the other half as Ben Dor (did I tell you he was taking the house?) wanted to move in. It was a sort of semi-removal, so of course I have been very busy. What do you think? Mr and Mrs Holliday are coming out in May: isn't it amusing? I wish you were.

12th April
From Tan Tur

Here we are again in this peaceful spot. I'm expecting Cliff and Prof. Abercrombie tonight. They have been to Haifa and Tabgha, and are coming back by way of Beisan. Nebi Musa has passed so far without trouble; so I need not really have left the house, but it's nice to be here. Tigger is sitting by me on a rug; he talks all the time; his sounds are numerous but unintelligible. He's rather a noisy baby, but it's nice noise.

If everything goes well, we're going to Petra next Sunday. Isn't it thrilling? Why aren't you here? Cliff and I and Prof. Abercrombie and Concannon will go. It seems too good to be true. I'm sure something will happen to stop me going.

On a visit to Petra

I must start this account from the beginning, then I shall not forget anything. We set off for Transjordania at seven in the morning, and proceeded to our meeting place, where all the baggage was strapped round the car: personal luggage, camp beds, stools, blankets, provisions and cooking tackle. We had decided not to go straight to Amman, but to go north and see Gerash first. We had picnic lunch just before reaching Gerash, by a little stream where it was green and cool. We then went on, and spent the afternoon examining the ruins which are quite extensive. There are colonnaded streets, a forum, theatre, temples and early Christian churches. The early Roman plan is very clearly marked out. They have excavated quite a lot recently, and the town is quite as interesting as Baalbec. We left for Amman at 4.30 and reached there just in time to have a walk around the town before dinner. It's not a bad little place, and boasts of one 'antiqua', the Roman theatre which was just opposite the hotel.

Next morning, all the men wore Arab headdress, guide and chauffeur included so, from a distance, we might have been a car full of Arabs. We saw two places of interest on the way: the Madeba mosaic, which was not as interesting as we expected, partly, I think, because the little boys of the village were so quarrelsome and kept fighting about who should show us the mosaic and get the bakshish. It's quite an amusing map, and shows more clearly on a good photograph than on the actual floor. Our next stop was Ma'Shatta, a Persian palace built of brick right in the middle of the desert, far away from everywhere. We met two Bedouins there who offered us camel's milk out of a filthy goat-skin. We declined with thanks.

In the afternoon, we took a side road to Kerak, where we intended to spend the night. It was a dull and monotonous ride, but worth going to see. Kerak was a very well fortified town of the crusaders, and must have been almost impossible to capture. It's terribly steep on all sides, and very high. We got a marvellous view of the Dead Sea from the castle. The castle and walls are very well preserved, but the town inside looks like a mass of ruins. Our visit must have been quite an event, because a large crowd of village boys was following us wherever we went: one of them spoke English and was very talkative. We have arranged to sleep at the Latin Monastery, and had a letter for the English Father in charge. We found him to be a young man from Liverpool: wasn't it amusing? He was very glad to see us, and the Professor has promised to go and see his people when we get back.

Our last journey was most monotonous, flat scrubby desert all the way. One or two things happened to relieve the monotony. We suddenly came upon a huge square of water, like a reservoir, originally Roman. It was full of water, and shepherds with flocks of sheep were all round the edge, drinking from goat skin bags. But what disturbed us was a poor black cow that had apparently fallen in and was swimming round and round the edge. No-one appeared to be taking much notice and if Cliff, Concannon and our guide had not assisted it out, I think the poor thing would have swum around until it died of exhaustion. The next episode was not so pleasant. We suddenly found our driver going dreadfully fast, and Abercrombie, who was dozing, was jerked against the side of the car and gave himself a terrible black eye. Apparently the driver had seen some Bedouin on horseback in the distance, and thought they might hold us up.

Towards four o'clock, we passed a spring coming out of rock, supposed to be the place where Moses struck the rock, and a little further on we reached the village of Wadi Musa (Moses's stream). The coming to the village was rather sensational. We had been going through very dull, flat country, rather dry and very uninteresting, when suddenly we turned the corner and saw a fertile little valley with trees and fields and, beyond, a most extraordinary outcrop of the most fantastic rock you can imagine. Great high jagged things, all bare and grey, most menacing. We left the car at Wadi Musa, packed the baggage on two mules and took horses. (I feel most safe on a horse until it gallops.) After a walk through the village, we entered the famous gorge. It is really all that one hears about it. The rock walls are terribly high, white at first and then they get the famous red colour, not only red but a sort of dark pink and blue in stripes, and sometimes looking like pink and blue marble. The colour is amazing, and quite indescribable. The passage between the rocks is so narrow that sometimes the horses had to paddle in the stream. We must have gone about half a mile before we got to the valley which is Petra.

It was nearly dark when we arrived, but we had just time to choose our caves and unpack our beds. Two small caves for bedrooms and a larger one for dining room and kitchen combined. Our table was a flat stone on stone legs, and our chairs four small stones. We had picked up a cook in Ma'an, and he served quite a nice hot dinner. We had two whole days to see Petra, and had a long walk each day; fortunately it was cloudy weather, and very pleasant for climbing: we should have found it very hard work in the sun. The first climb was to the temple (I won't describe it, I'll send a photo) the second to an altar of sacrifice. This last was over 6500 feet up, and the climb was terribly steep, quite precipitous in parts. There

Eunice outside her cave at Petra

Petra

Petra

had originally been flights of stairs, but these had been worn away and were just a slippery slope. For each walk we had an armed guide or a policeman. The guide was a wild Bedouin with curls, and very well armed with a rifle, revolver and dagger (well-sharpened, and which he used to pick his teeth or extract thorns from his bare toes) and a belt full of ammunition. When we got to a particularly steep climb, he used to burst into a song to cheer us on our way.

We had one unexpected interest, and that was locusts. The whole valley was full of them, not the adult flying kind, but the little hoppers, about an inch long. There were thousands of them all over the ground and massed at the bottom of each bush. We burnt several bushes, but there were so many that it didn't seem worthwhile. We walked on them all the way up to the Place of Sacrifice and, when we went under the rocks, they dropped onto our heads. Their hopping makes a noise just like a sharp shower of rain.

Now I must tell you about our adventurous journey home. We left Petra about 6.30, and had started from Wadi Musa just before nine. After we left Ma'an, we found, to our horror, that it had been raining in Transjordan all the time we had been in Petra and the road, which is only a summer track, was pure mud. We got on alright in the morning, and had a rather scanty lunch on a very windy little railway station. In the afternoon it started to rain, the car was skidding about all over the place, and twice we had to push it out of the mud. Eventually we stuck, just when it was beginning to get dark. We were twenty miles from Amman and it was pouring with rain. Anyway, the guide said there was a village about half a mile away where there might be a telephone, or we might stay the night with the Headman, who was a Christian from Salt.

So, we collected our essentials from our bags: biscuits, chocolate – and fortunately Cliff had a big flashlight – and set off through the mud. We were just beginning to think that the village was a myth (or mirage might be more appropriate) when we saw bright lights on the road, and these turned out to be two RAF tenders. One of them was going to Ma'an, but the second only to Zizia, to pick up a man who had come down in an aeroplane. He said we could all get in and go with him, and then he would take us back to Amman. So we climbed in. It was quite roomy and warm. We collected our bags from the car, which we passed on the way, and changed into clean socks. The two tommies driving were very cheerful, with good strong Lancashire accents. We were two hours getting to Zizia, where we collected the two aeroplane men and were regaled with bottles of beer. We started for home at ten, having collected blankets and square mattresses (biscuits). Cliff made me up a bed with some of these on the floor, and I slept the whole way home. We knocked up the hotel at 3 o'clock in the morning. The proprietor had quite given us up, and was very surprised to see us. Two other parties were on the way, and we don't know yet what happened to them. One party consisted of four American ladies from Beirut.

Anyway, it was all most unexpected: we thought of heat, but never of rain at this time of year. I only hope it killed the locusts, but I'm afraid not, because from Amman to Jericho the road, in part, was so thick with them that they crackled under the car wheels as we went along. We were very lucky not be stranded in some Arab village, and we've none of us caught cold or feel any the worse. We would have given a good deal for some hot soup when we arrived, after breakfast at six. We had a very sparse lunch and no tea or dinner, except for cheese and biscuits. But, as the Professor remarked, 'These people do a certain amount for you, but not too much'. All that was available was whisky and soda, and I think, under the circumstances, even Mother might have fallen for my inch of neat whisky before I went to bed. I came home to find Timothy with mumps, but he is quite better now. So it's all over, unless Cliff gets it.

6th May
To Elizabeth

I am sorry you weren't with us (except on the last day) but I am very glad we didn't go last summer. It was fairly warm the day we went through the desert, warm enough to make one realise how very hot and exhausting it would have been: just miles and miles of flat scrubby country, with nothing at all to relieve the monotony (and we did hope to see an ostrich). Another reason I am glad that we did not go out of the season is because there does seem to be some danger from

Bedouins and the tribe of cave-dwellers there called Budalas; and, if you remember, we were told there is no police protection in the summer.

Professor Abercrombie goes on Thursday morning. We are going to the luncheon in his honour tomorrow, and he has invited us and Concannon to have dinner with him tomorrow night. Last night, there was a big dinner given for him by the Town Planning Commission (all men). Cliff made a speech, which I hear was excellent… I haven't had a minute to breathe since we moved. All the rush to get ready before Mr and Mrs Holliday came has been simply terrific. Bethlehem workmen are the worst I have struck yet for prevarication. We are not straight yet, but presentable. Mr and Mrs Holliday came yesterday and like the house. Please forward this home as soon as you can, so they will know we are alive. I've never been so rushed in my life.

23rd May

I've been busy every minute since we got in the house, and have had to use my spare time being sociable to my visitors. Cliff is busy too, as Abercrombie took up a lot of his time, so he is rather behind with his work. Fortunately, Mrs Holliday is quite content to stay in the house and garden, and Mr Holliday wanders about Jerusalem and makes friends with all and sundry. We are enjoying this house immensely: it's lovely, and so cool. We have had the first fruits of our garden, mulberries, stewed, and walnuts, which I am going to pickle.

14th June
Haifa

We are here two days; Cliff has a meeting about the harbour. Tomorrow, we are going to Tabgha to show our visitors the Sea of Galilee. The children are to be at home with the bodyguard of retainers. There is Miss Kenyon and Sophie. Miss Miller is going to sleep in the house, and there are Jameel and Ahmed in the kitchen. I think I told you I had Cliff's office boy, Jameel, for half days. I now have him all the time. He is very good: he cooks beautifully and is most reliable. He can go to the market, or go messages, in fact do anything. He is a most faithful sort of person. Ahmed helps him and does the cleaning. I have had him for a long time too. He gets in a temper occasionally and says he wants to leave, but usually recovers in time… I will send you some Jordan water. Mr and Mrs Holliday sail on about the 2nd of July. They are enjoying their stay. We had a good time in Tiberias, but it was very hot. We came home in record time. We left Tabgha at 6.00 and were in Jerusalem by 11.00. We came early because it was the day when three of the rioters from Safed were going to be hanged, and we expected trouble on the road. However, all was quite, although the Arabs were very angry. I think they ought to consider themselves very lucky that they got off so easily. None of the Hebron murderers was hanged.

Mr and Mrs Holliday have stood the heat and change very well: Mr Holliday was 60 last March. We went to the Jordan, and Mr Holliday collected a large bottle of Jordan water to take home... I've had my new nurse for four days. I think you would like her, but she must be 60. She is inclined to be 'missionary', very patient and gentle but quite firm. I think she is rather nice, but I can't help feeling she will find it too hard work. She has been to Australia, New Zealand, Canada and California, and now she is determined to stay here for a few years. I have a suspicion she is waiting for the end of the world. Anyway, she says she learned to swim when she was 50, has a cold bath every morning, and makes Paul, John and Timothy have one too.

8th July
From Bodell's, Port Said

We have had some rather terrible news. Mr Holliday died on Saturday. He was not well when he left on Friday, but on Thursday night the doctor said it was slight influenza aggravated by the heat. He advised him not to travel, but as they were very anxious to go (Mr Holliday had some business to see to) the doctor said it would probably be all right. However, he developed pneumonia with startling rapidity, and died of double pneumonia and jaundice on Saturday night. Mrs Holliday had a dreadful journey; she got him on the boat, and then had to get him off again and to the English Hospital. The funeral had to be Sunday, and we couldn't get here until Sunday night. All we could do was to wire the head of the Bible Society to help her.

15th July

We got back here on Friday morning feeling rather limp. There are some nice letters waiting for Cliff, but those wretched Scottish Memorial people are the limit: there is not a word of sympathy from any of them. All they do is simply pester Cliff for work he has not been able to do. Really, some people are hard. I was in the office for a little this morning, and there was a continuous stream of people coming in all the time. We shall have to try to get a holiday somewhere in September. Cliff is working until 7.30 without coming home for lunch, and I don't think it is good in the summer. However, perhaps this rush won't last too long.

27th September
Haifa

The harbour is going on apace; they seem to work all day and all night. It is quite brilliant to see Haifa at night from the top of Mount Carmel here. The boats are lit up on the water, and look like a carnival. The weather is perfect. I am sitting in a little shelter under a bougainvillia, and there is enough cool breeze to make it really pleasant.

6th October

We had a good time in Haifa, and all feel better for it. We had a day picnic at Athlit, an old site with a ruined crusader castle on the shore. The sea and sand were lovely there. Another day we went to the 'aeroplane boat' (Paul's name for it) and it was most interesting. The whole ship was covered with one immense deck, and immediately underneath was a hangar for twenty aeroplanes. They were lined up in rows, and had their wings folded back. They are taken on deck by a lift. We went up and down several times. We went all over the ship, and Paul and John had an ice cream at the soda fountain and went into the engine room.

24th October

In six months or so, we shall be home, I hope; the time will go very quickly, for us anyway, as there will be so much to do. Cliff seems to want me to come first. I've just heard a dreadful story. The non-religious Jews have a football team here which always plays on Saturdays. The religious Jews offered them £50 a month not to play on the Sabbath. They took the money all through the summer and, now the football season has started, they have written to say they are going to play on Saturdays again. Isn't it the limit? The first match is tomorrow, and the Orthodox Jews are going to protest, so there will probably be a row.

29th October

Our latest baby is Jameel's. He has a wife and one little girl, aged three. Unfortunately, this second one is a girl too. Jameel's mother is very distressed, and insists that he gets another wife at once that can produce sons. Anyway, Jameel doesn't care what kind of baby it is, and says one wife is enough: he is a Moslem and could have more if he wanted.

20th November

I forgot to tell you about John. He was brought home from school in the middle of one morning with a black eye and a very small puppy. The eye he had got from falling on a tent peg, and the puppy was given to him by a boy at school for being so brave. He had a nasty bruise, but luckily the eye itself was not hurt. I put Pond's on at once, and the swelling soon went down, though his eye was nearly shut for two days. The puppy is minute, and John adores it; so does Timothy. I wish you could see them playing together.

Cliff is spending all his time on the Scottish Memorial. It is to be opened a week on Sunday, St Andrew's Day. Mr Hill arrived this week. He was the man we stayed with in Edinburgh. He is to be the resident Minister for the first year. He is a nice old man, we like him very much. He is going to christen Timothy.

I am sorry the Maugers have gone. Cliff will miss Mr Mauger, for they exchanged ideas. Oh, it is a pity we can't have better people in the Government.

I was with Mrs Cook yesterday, and she told me about an old Arab she knows, who knew Allenby and his people. If one mentions the English to him, he says: 'English? These are not English, the English came but they went away again: they will come back soon.' I am afraid that the Arabs and Jews are getting a very bad impression of us. We are waiting to hear what becomes of the White Paper. I've heard, from two sources, that the Arabs are preparing a much greater massacre, about two or three years hence, if they are not satisfied with Government policy.

The Scottish Memorial Church

The Scottish Memorial opening was very nice. Lots of people were there, and all admired the church. I think it is beautiful. It is plain stone, and the one colour is blue: blue stained glass windows, blue (and gold) cloth on the altar table. I am sending you a copy of the service.

7th December

Timothy was christened in the Scottish Church this morning by Mr Hill. He was very good. The service was short, and Mr Hill let Cliff hold him whilst he baptised him, so he didn't cry at all. He seemed very interested in the whole proceedings, and had quite a lot of water on his head. The water we had drawn from Jacob's well at Nablus when we came from Haifa. It was beautifully clear, and was put into a cut glass bowl, as the font is not yet ready.

23rd December

This afternoon should have been the Government House party, but Robin Chancellor is in bed with a cold, so it has been postponed until Saturday. They rang up from Government House to say they had just heard there was a small Timothy, and would he like to go? I shall take him. He likes noise and other children.

We are invited to the inauguration of the new King David Hotel. It is a most marvellous hotel of a new kind for Jerusalem. Tourists are paying £2 to £3 a day there.

12

1931

Eunice and Cliff went on leave in the late spring and summer, Eunice going first with John and Timothy, Cliff and Paul following overland, calling at a number of European cities. There is a lot of reference beforehand to the state of affairs in England, where the depression had begun to bite. It is likely that Cliff assessed the job market when he was home, and didn't much like what he saw. At any rate, they returned to Palestine in October. In the background must also have been an assessment of the policy statement from the British Government following the 1929 riots and the Commission Report which, while recognising the problems of the Arab population in agreeing that the Jewish immigration should be slowed down, did not in fact achieve that result. A census for Palestine, taken this year, showed a population of nearly 760,000 Muslims, 174,000 Jews and 91,000 Christians. At a rough census, made in 1923, there had been 590,000 Muslims, nearly 84,000 Jews and 73,000 Christians. During the next five years, another 190,000 Jews were admitted. The rise in the Jewish population did cause concern, but did not lead to the threat of riots, and things remained fairly quiet.

So, yet again, Cliff and Eunice's decision to return home was put off. The Bethlehem house was proving a success, and Cliff took Paul and John into school every day. Ellie, a young German girl, was taken on to help look after Timothy and the boys generally. Life was fairly peaceful.

※

2nd January
On New Year's Eve, we joined a party at a supper dance at the new King David Hotel. It is a lovely place, much more luxurious and better run than anything Jerusalem has had before. The management was very lavish with et ceteras, and we were provided, in the course of the evening, with crackers (in abundance), squeakers, whistles, paper hats, balloons, rattles, streamers, little balls et cetera. I came home with quite a collection of oddments for Paul and John.

We went to Bethlehem on the Greek Orthodox Christmas Eve. It was interesting, because their service is in the real old basilica, and it looked beautiful, with the contrast between the hundreds of little coloured lamps against the dark wall and old grey columns. Cliff and I went the Sunday after the Scottish Church was opened, and it occurred to us that on two successive Sundays we had been in the newest and the oldest churches in the world.

27th January

We had the great Mohammed Ali's funeral on Friday. I expect you know that he was brought from England to be buried in the Haram area. I didn't go to see the procession, as I was afraid I might not be able to get back to Bethlehem, there was such a crowd. Cliff watched it from the bank. He said the brother was walking in front of the coffin, bowing like a king. There was a terrific crowd of Arabs in the town, and Jameel told me that hundreds wanted to come from India, but the Government would not let them. It seems Mohammed Ali was a great friend to Palestine, and sent a lot of money to the distressed Arabs after the riots.

20th February

I don't think I shall come home in April, not unless Cliff turns really obstinate. I'd rather wait and come altogether. It's possible, too, that we may come back here for a little. Everyone writes how bad conditions are in England. We had a letter from Mr Mauger, and he doesn't sound too cheerful. Also, Cliff has several jobs in the offing and, if they materialise, it seems absurd to let them go. If it weren't for Father and Mother I should be glad to stay. Part of the garden is just fields of yellow and purple flowers. Tigger sits down in the middle of them, and you can hardly see him. And we've got almond trees in bloom all over the hillside. Cliff is busy showing Jerusalem to Mr Chubb, of Chubb's safes.

We had a great argument with our landlord last week, for he was determined to plough up all the garden. The Arabs think that if they don't plough up the fields, the fruit trees will die. He had promised to leave us the part immediately in front and behind the house for the children to play in but, as you know, promises mean nothing, so up he came with his plough. I argued with him, so he turned his back on me and I said the rudest thing I knew in Arabic which was 'mafish mukh', which means he has no brains. He raised his hand above his head and said he had brains up to heaven! Fortunately, an American lady called on me that afternoon whose Arabic is fluent, so she tackled the landlord whilst I held the horse, and the landlord was too polite to interfere. Anyway, we stopped him for the afternoon, and when Cliff came, he rang up the District Officer in Bethlehem and said would he talk to Mr Shukri Nassar. So that's that, so far. We have some exciting times with our landlord: it is really a family of five brothers, and the one I tackled that afternoon happens to be the worst of the lot.

I hope you are not too disappointed that we're not coming for good yet. We really haven't enough money saved to keep us indefinitely, in case Cliff doesn't get a job. And we can't start a private practice without a good deal of capital. Besides, as Cliff's got more buildings here, it would be foolish to refuse.

24th March

John and Cliff returned safely from Gaza, having driven about nine hours on dreadfully bad roads. John was tired but happy, having been very good, and eaten a most tremendous lunch. He brought home a petrol tin full of sand and a box of chocolates presented to him by the Mayor of Gaza. They had one mishap, when the car went into a trench that was right across the road, and the back wheel got stuck. Fortunately, a lot of Bedouins were passing, and they all pushed from behind and got it out. One pushed his head through the back of the hood.

3rd April

The children will have quite a lot of Easter gifts. Their first present was a pet lamb. Cliff and I are both longing to see real green country, lanes and stiles et cetera. I can't believe it's eight years since we spent a summer in England. I am afraid Father is rather optimistic about affairs in England. Concannon has just come back from leave. He saw lots of people we know, and they all sent messages to us to stay here, as there was no work. He had lunch with one architect who said afterwards, 'I've nothing to do, let's go to the pictures.'

9th April

Did you see the eclipse? It caused a great sensation amongst the fellaheen. We showed it to Gabriel, our little Bethlehem boy, thinking he would be interested, but he was more than interested, he was frightened to death. He kept saying, 'No good, no good.' He explained, in Arabic, that the shadow was red, signifying blood. Strangely enough, it was the night before the Moslem Nebi Musa procession and the day after Passover, when anything might have happened. After a little while, he went inside and returned with a lamp and a prayer book. He put the lamp in the middle of the garden and knelt down on the grass facing the moon, then proceeded to say his prayers, crossing himself all the time. After that, he came and asked if he could go to church: it was ten o'clock. He told me the next morning that he had got home at two in the morning, and that all Bethlehem had been praying in church. Jameel told me later that Moslems had been similarly employed in the mosque. There has been a terrible lot of traffic on the road today, bus-loads of Moslems going back to Hebron after Nebi Musa and more bus-loads of Bethlehemites going to Jerusalem.

It is just a year since we were in Petra... Concannon is just back from England, where he saw Professor Abercrombie. He may possibly take over our house when we come home. We would like someone to live in it. Jameel will stay on, of course, and I should like to keep Gabriel. He is a little slow, but a good boy, and he gets on with Jameel.

To Elizabeth

I hope that you are prepared to visit us in 1932? This is the year, I believe, when the great earthquake is to divide the Mount of Olives in two, and let the Mediterranean into the Jordan Valley. You might see it, or are you not of the chosen? Cliff was told the other day that only picked people were coming to Palestine now. I don't think much of the picker!

16th April

I was interested in your dream of me and Timothy coming home, because one morning we had a new idea. It is for me to come home first with Timothy and John, and leave Cliff and Paul to keep house together. They would leave a few weeks later, and come home slowly overland - seeing things. I think it's a good idea. It would be interesting for Cliff, good for Paul, and we should have more time with you. Paul is old enough to be left, and is a very good companion.

Whit

We are staying at Tan Tur for two days. Cliff has gone to Suez. He has been sent by the Government to inspect the petroleum stores, I suppose with a view to advising on the pipeline. He did not want to leave us alone in the house, as it is rather lonely. It's a nice change, even if only next door, so to speak. Tigger (Timothy) has taken a great fancy to the little church here. It has very brightly-coloured windows, really rather gaudy, all red, blue and yellow. He loves them, also life-size images of Jesus and Mary. He seems to have got a little mixed about them, for today he said, 'Dat Jesus, and dat Mary, Mary had a little lamb!' He has just drawn a very good picture of the church and, when he had finished it, he said, 'church got legs? No, got ground', so he drew a straight line at the bottom. The Mother Superior here is so kind and well-meaning, she has just been up to give Paul some weak tea, and with a bottle of brandy! She suggested that half a teaspoon would keep up his strength. I don't suppose Cliff will find much of interest in Suez, but John has ordered a bottle of Red Sea water with a baby shark in it, and Paul suggested a barrel of oysters, whether for the oysters or the mother of pearl, I don't know.

After leave in England

26th October

At last, I can settle down to write a letter about our arrival. We left the ship at eleven in the morning and, as we had a day to spend at Port Said, we went to Bodells – a nice quiet hotel on the sea-front – where we took a room. After lunch, Tigger went to sleep and Cliff took some flowers to the cemetery (to his father's grave). We left at 6.00 and reached Kantara about 7.00. We had some dinner on the station and watched the *City of Paris* go through the canal. The Jerusalem train came in about twenty past nine, so we settled the children down for the night, even though we were not due to leave until eleven. We were all awake by 6.00. There was a car waiting for us at Ludd to take us home: this saved an hour. When we got to the gate, we found it all decorated with greenery and coloured paper. There were streamers flying and paper twisted around the bars: it was Jameel's welcome home. The house was spotlessly clean, all the beds made, plenty of food in the house, including a joint of beef for dinner!

10th December
From Casa Nova, Nazareth
Here we are in Nazareth, and staying just across the road from the supposed house of the Virgin Mary. Father Hunt has come with us, and he and Cliff are surveying the site and old remains of various churches. It is there that they propose to build a big new church on the foundations of the fourth century one. This is a hospice for pilgrims, clean and bare. The food is curious, Italian, and we have macaroni soup for every meal, and lots of eggs. We are leaving this afternoon and going to Tabgha.

14th December
I'm sitting under the pine trees on Carmel, with all Haifa Bay below me. I'm beginning to like Carmel as well as Tabgha, but not quite. All the sisters seem like friends, and are so anxious to do anything they can to make us happy. Ellie, Tigger and I have been in the woods, where we've dug up lots of cyclamen roots to take home. It looks as if there will be hundreds of flowers here in a few months. I've always heard that Carmel is wonderful in the spring.

You must come on the seaplane. We saw it land on Galilee. We had just arrived in Tiberias, and were parked in the square, when suddenly everyone began running to the shore, and it sailed almost over our heads onto the lake. It was most thrilling, especially when we thought that you might land that way, one day.

13

1932

1932 marks ten years for the family in Palestine, a long stay for two young people, but it shows the opportunities for Cliff in his career, and the interest in life out there for them both. In preparing a plan for Jerusalem, working on the archaeology of the old city and designing several new buildings, Cliff had a range of experience that would have been impossible to get at home. In having the children – and this year a fourth – Eunice and Cliff brought up a family in happy homes and surroundings of great interest.

But after ten years, Eunice writes that Cliff is fed up with Palestine, and wants to come home. Apart from the depression, and Abercrombie saying that jobs were difficult to get, money was a problem. They had saved none, and needed some to see them through a first spell in England. The question of schools for Paul and John was also becoming important, and I surmise that they began to make serious plans for a return during this year.

The fourth boy, Robin, was born in November. As Eunice's doctor worked in Tel Aviv, she decided to have the baby there, and stayed with Ellie and the three boys in a pension run by a Hungarian Jewess. It was near the sea, and memories of it are pleasant enough, apart from some of the food. Tel Aviv seems to have been quite a welcome change from Jerusalem for Eunice, especially the pavement cafes and general activity. Cliff had to travel between Tel Aviv and Jerusalem for a month, sometimes with Paul and myself. I remember being frightened that we would have to travel to Tel Aviv at night if the baby was born then, on roads still threatened by brigands, in my mind at any rate. However, Robin was born quickly and easily, and no problem arose.

There were other new events during the year. Cliff had to visit the Dead Sea, where ideas of a pleasure resort were beginning. A new Abyssinian Coptic Church was begun in Jericho and, on a lighter note, Sybil Thorndyke and Company came out and played Bernard Shaw's St Joan. Elizabeth planned to come out again, but seems to have been short of money. Eunice's letter includes information on four cheap ways to travel from England to Palestine. Elizabeth still had her post lecturing at Royal Holloway College, and was to spend here whole career there, but she also did a lot of travelling. The projected trip to

Bethlehem was to be her fourth to Palestine, and clearly Eunice was much looking forward to it. Perhaps she found life in the country too quiet. She always preferred towns.

4th January

We had a lovely Christmas and New Year, and I had a thrill on Sunday. We went down to the Dead Sea (there is a marvellous road now, not the old track) where Cliff had a meeting on the spot about this new pleasure resort, and after picnic lunch we were taken on the Dead Sea in a speed boat, right down on the other side to the hot springs. The rocks were just like Petra, and there were little crannies and gorges filled with palm trees and the water was really hot. I did want to bathe, and there was a lovely calm bay with a little beach which would be perfect for camping. The boat belongs to the salt people: Major Tulloch's son drives it. It's thrilling, dashing through the water at about forty miles an hour. We did touch forty four once, but even fifteen is exciting. I would not have missed it for anything. The Dead Sea shore is quite changed, there are lots of houses and tents and great white fields of salt. By the way, Major Tulloch told us that the Children of Israel never went into Sinai, and the Red Sea is a mistranslation, and means reed sea, which is the marshy land all about the coast near El Arish.

2nd February
To Elizabeth

I am glad you are so enthusiastic about flying, because now you will surely come next spring. I expect that when the Haifa harbour is finished, the aeroplanes will come down there instead of Galilee. The sudden squalls – which disturbed Peter when he was fishing – seem just as upsetting to the aeroplanes: the waves sometimes prevent them from taking off. The land ones, which come from Cairo, land at Samak.

We have had a very cold and much too dry winter so far. We haven't a quarter of the rain we need and the wet season is half over. It's very serious, and the municipality haggle over the price of bringing water up from a spring near Jaffa. There was a notice in the paper to say that no water was to be used for building purposes after 1st May. So it doesn't look very cheerful for architects does it? There are rumours of other jobs in the offing. A new office block Cliff is doing is half way up, but Cliff says he is fed up with Palestine, and wants to come home, but we need to save up a fair amount of money to keep us at home before we come.

17th February

I think I missed a week in writing home. I was very busy. It was the Moslem Feast of Ramadan, and so Jameel and the other boy (called, strangely, Ramadan) had a holiday. They went off on Sunday, and did not come back until Wednesday. And what made me more busy was that on Sunday afternoon it began to snow! We had a week of rain which ended in hail and snow and a great wind. All our water was frozen, but fortunately we had anticipated this and filled the bath the night before. It didn't snow for long, but we had frost for about five days. What upsets me most is that all my nasturtiums are dead, and I had planted hundreds.

10th March

I have to walk to Bethlehem this morning. I hardly ever go there, but Uncle Percy sent Paul a money order, and sent it to Bethlehem post office... The bank is to be opened on Monday. Cliff showed members of the press over it yesterday, and is supposed to be showing members of the Architectural Society over this afternoon. The Dramatic Society are doing the Pirates of Penzance, and Cliff and Thomas Concannon have been asked to do the scenery... The bank is open. Cliff said the first morning it was very amusing to watch the general public using the swing door. It's a circular revolving one and, except for the King David and Palace Hotels, the only one in Jerusalem. Several people got bangs in the back because they did not get out quickly enough; others didn't get out at all, but revolved back into the vestibule!

6th April

We saw Sybil Thorndyke in *St Joan* last night, and enjoyed it very much. It was lovely to see a real play. She has her entire London company here, and they are going on to Australia. We were only going to see her once, but Thomas Concannon has invited us to see *Milestones* tonight. There is a matinee of *St Joan* today, and Ellie and Eriak have gone: I lent them the book, so I hope they will be able to follow it. It is the first play that Ellie has ever seen. Clara Butt had a poor reception: there were only about 35 people at the first concert. She was so upset, she sent out one hundred complimentary tickets for the second night, as she didn't like singing to empty chairs. It was foolishly arranged: the tickets were very expensive, and it was held at the King David Hotel so, of course, the ordinary Jewish population who like music could not go.

3rd May

Cliff is moving his office next week, from Connaught House to a set of rooms in an office block he built. I have been helping him to clear up, and Mother would be horrified at the amount of stuff we have thrown away. We may still be turned out of our house, but we are struggling hard to stay. Our landlords are so slippery to deal with and won't sign the contract, so we don't feel at all safe. We shall not like leaving the garden, after having put so much work into it.

11th May

Now, I wonder if your second sight, as regards my children, has told you that I am having my baby after all? I am very well, and we are very pleased because I don't think I could face having a child in England, and we did want to make one more attempt to have a daughter. I am sorry my doctor is in Tel Aviv, but I think, in spite of it, I shall go there, because I don't want to change doctors, and I should like Sister Jenny, now I know her so well. Now I must write to Mrs Holliday and tell her the news. She will be worried… she thinks children are so expensive.

22nd June

Cliff had to go to Jericho to see his Abyssinian Church foundations on Saturday, and took Paul and John. The thought of it made me feel hot. They came home all sticky – more than sticky – and had to hop under the cold shower to get cool.

5th July

We all went to Jericho one day last week. There was a cool breeze blowing, so it wasn't too hot. Cliff and Paul went on to the site of the Abyssinian Church, but John, Tigger and I stayed in the garden of a Franciscan Monastery in Jericho, a lovely shady garden full of vines and banana trees. The old Father there was very hospitable, brought us chairs and great bunches of fresh grapes, and later bottles of lemonade and lager beer. We had taken our sandwiches for tea. Paul and Cliff called for us about six, Paul carrying a melon given him by the Abyssinian Bishop. We went home laden with a big bag of grapes, a melon, a bunch of bananas, several plants, a paw paw and one enormous onion (we weighed it when we got home, and it weighed two and a half pounds). They were all presents from Father Jerome. Cliff and Paul had to go again yesterday afternoon to some sort of stone-laying ceremony. Cliff, Paul and the Bishop laid the stones, and Paul got another melon!

We are having to give up cultivating our garden. We only water tomatoes and a few special things, for water is getting very scarce now. Fortunately, the Government is getting down to the problem, at last, and we hope to have a permanent supply, sometime.

19th July
To Elizabeth

Of course we shall be delighted if you come in February. I'll enquire about quick cheap ways. Elise Abraham came out once in five days for about ten pounds… John coloured the picture of British children in the book you sent, but the poor child did all the fields light brown instead of green. You can't blame him, when you consider our landscape here. The effect of Palestine on the child mind is very unexpected. When I told the children that Mr Scott was dead, Paul said at once, 'Who shot him?'

23rd August

We have just received the book which the Liverpool students have compiled for Prof. Reilly on the occasion of his 25th year at the school. It is a collection of drawings and photos of work done by students. Cliff's Scottish Church is honoured with first place in the selection on building.

15th September

I have had to sack my second boy Ramadan; he got too uppish and quarrelsome with Jameel. I've got a smaller boy now from Jameel's village. He has never worked in a house before, but he's not bad. Of course, he sweeps round things instead of under, but he will soon learn if he is sent back often enough!

28th September

We had a pleasant day in Tel Aviv yesterday. Cliff had a meeting, and I took the children down to the shore to bathe. When Cliff came, we left them with Ellie and went to look for suitable rooms to stay in next month. We decided on Pension Moscowitz, a nice house near the sea. It is Jewish of course, but many English stay there. What chiefly appealed to us was Mrs Moscowitz herself, a kind, sympathetic and motherly person who seemed quite equal and willing to take charge of the whole family when I went to hospital.

I wonder if you have any of my Beatrix Potter books in good condition that you could send out? John has one and loves it, and is always asking me for more. We took Paul and John to the pictures last week. We saw 'The Battle of Balaclava' and 'The Charge of the Light Brigade'. They had read the poem at school and knew all about it. I hope it brought home the horrors of war. It was certainly very tragic. Even so, John asked me in the middle 'Would you like to be in a fight like that?'

We took our puppy Binga to Jaffa and threw her in the sea. She is enormous, just like a toy pup, all white and fluffy. She had a good time trying to bite the legs of the Jewesses who were strolling up and down the beach!

3rd October

Cliff has been busy this week. The British police are doing a play, and asked Cliff to do the scenery for them. He has done practically the whole thing himself, with a little help from the police carpenter and Thomas Concannon sometimes. On Saturday, he went for the day and took Paul with him. Fortunately, they took old clothes, because they came back speckled all over with paint, hair and all. John and Tigger were by themselves, but they play excellently together. They were very quiet for a long time, so I looked out into the garden and saw that they had lit a little bonfire. I learned afterwards that they had taken potatoes from the kitchen, which they roasted and ate. John is never at a loss for an idea.

13th October

We go to Tel Aviv next week. I don't know how long Cliff and the children will stay. It all depends on me and, so you know, my babies are always late, unfortunately.

19th October
Pension Moscowitz

Here we are safe and sound. The doctor says I shall be another week at least, so I must just be patient. It's a smallish baby, but opinions are divided as to whether it is boy or girl. However, as I feel very well I can enjoy a holiday by the sea, which is good for us all. Cliff brought us down on Sunday and stayed until this morning, when he returned to Jerusalem with Paul.

20th October
To Elizabeth
Pension Moscowitz

We are enjoying Tel Aviv, but it is quite a different sort of life to Jerusalem; it's not like Palestine at all, more like a seaside resort which could be anywhere. We, personally, create a sensation by building sand castles et cetera on the shore every day; we are the only people who build with sand, and the shore is packed with children, its amazing. You wouldn't believe the number of people who stop to admire Ellie's little models of houses, which she makes with Paul and John. Earnest young men stop and point them out to each other; mothers show their children, and some children stay for ages to watch. What they would do on the usual English beach, I don't know. I can't understand it, unless it's because these Jews come from Russia or central Europe and have never seen sand before, and don't know its possibilities. Ellie makes very good houses by instinct. By the way, she will be a great asset to you, for she adores collecting – anything – pebbles, shells, plants, creepy crawlies. She will play for hours with a praying mantis (when she ought to be mending socks). It is quite exasperating at times, but very amusing for the children. Yesterday, she wanted to get Tigger up from his afternoon sleep to show him a funny coloured cat he hadn't seen before. She has the patience of Job and the good temper of an angel and that's why I keep her.

Did I tell you that there has been a big split-up in the American Colony? There was a big row with the heads of it, and most of the young and middle aged people left altogether. It's composed now of the old dears and a very few young ones. There are only two children in the colony, I believe, so I suppose it will gradually die out.

4th November

It's the 4th and I was due in hospital on the nineteenth of October!... We spend a lot of time eating ice cream... There are lots of open air cafes here with little tables on pavements, continental fashion. It is very pleasant, and so easy to walk. Jerusalem is all hilly and rocks, but Tel Aviv is like Southport, flat wide streets and plenty of shops. We get much more exercise there than we do at home. Cliff has lost weight since he came, much to his joy! Tigger is as brown as a berry and so happy. He is as good-tempered as ever. John is still very thin, but well in spite of that. Paul is strong and healthy and growing taller. What a blessing it is to have healthy children.

7th November
From Cliff

Patrick, that's a tentative name – please say if you don't like it – arrived on Sunday night at 10.30. I was with Eunice until 9.00. I sent you a cable on Monday morning. I'm afraid Lois is not to be, but we don't really mind. He was born well and strong, and Eunice is all right. It is too early to say what he looks like, but he weighed seven and a quarter pounds and has very rosy cheeks. He looks strong and healthy. I brought the children back today, they are so brown. Ellie and Lulu are here, so we shall be well looked after. The children saw the new arrival before leaving.

6th November

I've done it again! And I can say with perfect truth, I have four children, and not – as the Arabs would say – three children and a girl. Some people have been consoling, which is really rather comic as I don't care two hoots. Of course, I would have liked to have given Cliff a daughter, but he has not objected so far. All the Jews around me think it is splendid: as Doctor Danziger said to me, 'But why do you want a girl?' Mrs Ben Dor and Mrs Moscowitz have sent congratulations: both have four sons. Cliff and I had a most wonderful firework display on the 5th. We took a walk along the shore after dinner and saw the most marvellous lightning over the sea. It spread until it was all round us. Forks, zigzagging all over the place, and thunder. Miss Nixon said the child had better be called Thor! By the way we may change our minds about 'Patrick'. He doesn't seem like a 'Patrick'.

8th November
From Cliff
Professor Abercrombie is very pessimistic about conditions at home. He is more cautious than you are.

12th November
All was perfectly normal, except the child can say – with David Copperfield – I was born with a caul. Apparently, in Germany, this is considered very lucky. I don't know if it is in England, except sailors used to keep them in bottles for luck. He is a nice baby, red and brown: a John type of baby, small and very wide awake, with wide-open eyes which are always looking round. The children came to see me on Monday; I think of the three of them Tigger was the most impressed. He said at once 'Can I have it?' and wanted to take it home in the car... A little lizard has just run into my bedroom: he's rushing about the floor trying to catch flies, but I am afraid he's rather inexperienced.

13th November
From Cliff
Eunice has made such a quick recovery that Doctor Danziger thinks she will be able to come home on Thursday. Robin – for that's the baby's name now – is a fine fellow.

24th November
I am lying out in the sun and writing on my knee. I came home quite soon, after eleven days. Robin is very good and, being my fourth, is well trained and gives no trouble: I lie in the sun and sew. Tigger is a very good errand boy: he fetches and carries and takes messages to Jameel and Ellie. No, of course we don't mind what the child is. He's a very nice baby and we love him. It's nice to have a little one to play with again. When we had three, Cliff used to say, 'I wish there were six'. Last week, he remarked, 'I wish there were ten'. Everyone is condoling because of the expense, which makes him rather rattled. I had a visit from Mr Paul, the Abyssinian Consul; he brought flowers and a huge box of Damascus sweets... Everyone likes Robin: he really is an attractive baby, not skinny, and with a nice little head and just enough hair. He has bright eyes, like a Robin; Zelda was most surprised, she had never seen a baby so small, and yet so human-looking.

20th December
To Elizabeth
It is lovely to think you are coming in February. I gather you are staying until Easter. The Greek Easter is the same as our own this year. Now, about routes.

I don't see how it can be quick and interesting at the same time. There are four ways, from the quick-and-cheap point of view:

1 Train, London to Triest: 2 days; boat, Triest to Jaffa: 5 days. 7 days, cost £27.10 in all.
2 Train, London to Marseilles. Marseilles to Jaffa, boat. Costs about the same and takes about the same time.
3 Similar, but to Port Said.
4 Train, London to Toulon, £7. Boat, Toulon to Port Said, £10.

Now, about clothes: it's a little difficult, as April is such an erratic month, but I should say bring chiefly winter clothes. If it's not too much trouble, you will find your sheepskin jolly if you go out at night: I wear mine a lot. Do remember that Jerusalem houses are not built for winter: little house coats are essential. Bring a few summer things for Tabgha and Haifa. About hats, bring something that will stay on in a wind and doesn't mind the rain; bring strong shoes or wellingtons, our mud is terrific. The thin light macs one wears at home are no use here, for when it rains it is cold.

27th December

We had a lovely Christmas. Ellie went off on Christmas Eve, as her big celebration is then – in German fashion – and she didn't return until Christmas morning. Robin woke up at a quarter past six, so Cliff went in then to the children's room to find Paul and John had already emptied their pillow slips. Tigger slept on through the noise until after seven. Sister Jenny came on Christmas Eve: we were very glad to have her. On Christmas afternoon, we had a children's party, though the visitors consisted of three children and nine adults. However, as the fathers were even more child-like than the children, the party was quite a success! Robin was handed round after tea and behaved perfectly. Our last guest departed about half past seven, then we had dinner, with Paul and John staying up. Sister Jenny had to go back to Tel Aviv to be on duty by seven this morning. She said it was the first real Christmas she had had since she came to Palestine. She had always been amongst Jews before. I wished just one thing, that you could all have been here.

14

1933

I n February, Elizabeth made her fourth and final visit, staying in the Bethlehem house. Going home, she experienced her first Imperial Airways flight, and enjoyed it.

Shortly afterwards, the family moved from Bethlehem back to a house in the German Colony in Jerusalem. Eunice seems to have been glad to be back to a community and with the school nearby. The house itself was an interesting one, on various levels. Next to it was a building site full of bricks, unused, so it provided an ideal playground! All the family except Paul and Robin contracted scarlet fever, so these two were taken to the hospice at Tan Tur to stay and the house was put into isolation for some weeks. The Ethiopian Church in Jericho was opened in September, and the Ethiopian Queen came for the ceremonies. Elsewhere, Eunice writes that Cliff was given a gold medal and a tin of coffee beans but no fee. However, he did get the fee eventually.

This was the year in which Jewish immigration grew dramatically, with a surplus of more than thirty eight thousand over those who emigrated. Much was due to the rise of Nazi Germany. There were Arab riots in Jaffa, Haifa and Jerusalem, protesting to the Government about this and the sale of land, although much of this was done by the Arabs themselves. A force of special constables was again called up, and Cliff had to join. The riots, however, were not so bad as those in 1929, or those to come in 1936.

Cliff applied for a job in Johannesburg but did not get it, and there was still much agonising about a return to England. Although, with Professor Abercrombie coming out to work on the Haifa Foreshore Scheme there was plenty to do, much of the novelty and excitement had gone out of the country for them and a change was needed. They had been in Palestine for twelve years, knew much about its history and places, got on well with Arab and Jew and the many other races and nationalities, and had achieved a good deal. They were to spend another eighteen months in Jerusalem before at last returning to England.

22nd January
To Elizabeth

It was exciting to hear about your boat. Cliff, and probably Paul, will meet you at Lydda on the 28th. I do hope you will enjoy just living a quiet life here, wandering about the hills and picking flowers. Paul brought in the first anemones yesterday. The weather at the moment is heavenly, but we do pray for more rain. We went for a walk over the hills last week, and discovered Herod's aqueduct, which he built to bring water from Solomon's Pools to the Temple. The old Roman concrete is still there, so we have the old pipe in front of us and the new one at the back. Cliff has been busy on the map of Jerusalem. It is a pictorial map to go with a brochure which the YMCA is producing on its opening. They wanted it all in a hurry, and so he worked until 8.00 for ages with no rest. I'm keeping him going with Sanatogen— I am going to view a house this morning. We are contemplating moving into Jerusalem, but I am glad you will see what Professor Abercrombie called our Palazzo.

13th February

We are leaving our house. I am busy house hunting. We decided it is too far away now. Paul and John should go to school all day, and now there is a boys' club in connection with the YMCA where they can use the swimming pool, gym and playing fields. All their little friends go, and I think they should too. There is a club room there for little ones, and an occasional lecture. And it is difficult for me now with Robin. We don't like leaving this house, but the one hope we've got is very romantic. We haven't signed the contract yet, and you never know in this country, so I won't tell you anything about it until next week.

16th February

We are going to see our new house in Jerusalem this afternoon. It is a most romantic place. All little balconies and steps and odd-shaped rooms, like a fairy house. Cliff says it is a real architect's house. People say it is a mad house and that no servant will stay in it; and fancy having twenty seven steps! Jameel is thrilled to be living in Jerusalem and having electric light, so he won't care. We shall be in the midst of the English and German communities and quite near the school. Downstairs it has a lovely big sitting room, a very wee study, servant's room, store room and playroom. Up one flight of stairs are the dining room, kitchen and terraces, up a few more steps the bathroom, and higher still four bedrooms. All the rooms are odd shapes with queer vaulted ceilings, and many have balconies. The garden is quite big and shady with a big fig tree. We shall not be moving before Elizabeth comes.

Letters from Elizabeth on her fourth visit

1st March

It is perfectly lovely being here, and at last. I was met at Lydda by Cliff, Paul, John, Ben Dor and Jameel. They had been up since 4.00am. The ride, of about thirty miles, through Ramleh and Jerusalem to Bethlehem was lovely. The rough white limestone hills were sprinkled with red anemones, pink cyclamen, blue grape hyacinths and yellow wood sorrel, and a small pink thing like red campion, sheets of it. Tigger was a little shy at first, but it didn't last long. He is as nice as ever, so happy and good. He is longer and thinner, quite a different shape, more like a boy. He looks lovely from behind, so straight. Robin is perfectly lovely, and no trouble at all. It is like living in the Arabian nights living in this house. It is vast (the hall, which is half the sitting room, is seventeen and a half by five metres, and six great rooms lead off it). The dining room is downstairs and so are the kitchens. All the floors are marble. It is beautifully warm outside today, with some cloud, but they are longing for rain. I have never seen rain here. Paul, John and Cliff went off about 8.00 this morning, with lunch all packed up. They will come back about 5.00. I am writing on the verandah, looking out towards Bethlehem and the olive-clad hills; almond trees in blossom are scattered among the olives. Inside the house are great bowls of red anemones and jars of almond blossom.

4th March

Paul and I drove in with Cliff this morning and went off by ourselves for two hours. Paul had a haircut, and then took me through the old city as far as the Church of the Holy Sepulchre, pointing out things of interest, ie the little crosses the crusaders chipped on the face of the stones. He is a good guide.

7th March

I am taking Paul and John to the pictures this afternoon. Afterwards, we shall pick up a car at the Jaffa Gate. The drivers will know Paul and John; Cliff will be busy with meetings and interviews all the time we are in Haifa. When we go to Tabgha, he will be going to Tiberias, where he is planning something!

From Tabgha

The children love Tabgha. Beyond the garden, along the shore, is a grove of eucalyptus, willow and bananas, and a warm stream runs through it to the lake. There are overhanging cliffs that can be climbed, and shells and pebbles and turtles and fish in the water; it is altogether very exciting. The garden, too, is lovely, heavily scented with orange blossom, and there are date palms, acacias, mimosa, and bougainvillias, great purple splashes over the walls. There are green kingfishers, ducks, pigeons and seagulls (all pure white). The pigeons roost in a date palm for a dovecote, and there is a white pussy cat that Tigger loves.

19th March

We came home yesterday, Cliff, Eunice and Robin in the front, Paul, John and I in the back, plus countless bags, cameras, coats and rugs; four suitcases, a pram, a cot and bath tied on outside. It is a run of about one hundred and twenty miles, and very difficult driving. We were all rather stiff and tired towards the end, and had to sing hard to pass the time.

1st April

Before 8.00, we went off to the Bethlehem market, Cliff, Eunice, Paul, John and I, Jameel carrying a large basket. I wonder if you would have enjoyed it as much as you usually enjoy markets. It is such a surging mass of shepherds in sheepskin, sheep, goats (and some such very young ones), fellaheen, men with camels, mules or donkeys, women carrying great baskets of herbs or live chickens on their heads, handsome young and old Bedouin with daggers in their belts, Bethlehem women with high white headdresses, lots of children, blind men led by boys. I kept getting in people's way, and was constantly pushed on one side by a great Bedouin paw! We were all rather jostled. It was difficult to see who was selling and who was buying: some people were, of course, doing both. There were two rows of perfectly good stalls which were completely ignored. The fellaheen prefer squatting on the ground and spreading their goods around them. There were loaves, cakes and highly coloured sweets, lots of wild sage and other herbs. There were oranges, huge Jaffas, chickens, lambs, et cetera. There were stone jars and shoes made from old motor car tyres. There were horses being shod on the spot. We came back with a basketful of oranges and two live chickens. You ought to have seen Eunice bargaining for chickens! We were back about 9.00, and off to Jerusalem soon after. It's 2.30 now, and Cliff and Paul have gone to a football match; John and Timothy are playing in the garden with Ellie; Robin and Eunice are asleep… We are going to the movies tonight: Laurel and Hardy.

11th April

We are in the midst of festivals. The first was Nebi Musa. On Friday, Eunice and I watched the procession from the Austrian Hospice balcony. The King and Queen of the Belgians had chosen the same place, very unostentatiously. On Sunday morning, we watched a still larger procession, which was increased by the addition of the wild Hebron men and Bedouins, banners, dancing, singing, cymbals, drums, mounted police, sheiks and the Grand Mufti. We had thought of watching from the Citadel (HE was there). But we had a better place, which was the roof of a house belonging to an Arab boy, Abib, who once worked in

Cliff's office. We were opposite the Citadel and walls of Jerusalem. The crowd on and below the city walls was as interesting as the procession. There were vendors supplying food and drink, lemonade and water, lettuces, bread rolls, eggs, meat tarts, fruit, and sticky sweets, et cetera.

The second festival was Passover. We celebrated Passover at the Ben Dor's. I found it most interesting, but of course lacking the wild gaiety of the Nebi Musa. (Abib would have liked to have taken us to Nebi Musa, Moses's tomb in the wilderness, to see the thousands of men encamped there, all having walked there from their villages by way of Haram-es-Sherif. Food and drink was supplied by the Wafd, there for eight days.)

The third festival was Christians' Easter. On Thursday, we began with the Feet Washing Ceremony. On Friday the 'Holy Fire'.

Letters from Eunice

1st May

I wonder if you have seen Elizabeth, and heard all the news. We are getting slowly into the new house, but we still have to have a few cupboards made.

We are enjoying being here. It's new and amusing to be near people. The German Colony itself is just like a village, just a few little shops and people going shopping with string bags early in the morning. Paul and John go to school by themselves: they have found a short cut, so it only takes them a few minutes. Timothy started today: he is to go from 11.00 to 12.30 every morning. He liked it so much this morning that he wanted to go again this afternoon; Sophie came to see us yesterday; she has not seen Robin before, but the first thing she said was 'He is just like your sister'. I was delighted that someone else, besides me, saw the resemblance.

10th May
To Elizabeth

We were delighted to get your letter. I am so glad that you enjoyed flying. Timothy was so pleased with his PPC (*the postcard of the aeroplane in which Elizabeth flew home*) that he would not let me hold it to look at. We showed it to Jameel, and told him you went home in it, and he seemed quite startled... Timothy is missing you very much. He finds it very trying to have no-one sitting still to listen to his interminable conversations. He has to console himself with Binga, and the poor dog has a dreadful time. She suffers it like a martyr, only too glad to have any sort of attentions.

29th May

The Queen of Abyssinia has not yet arrived. She has been coming for months. I have been making the top of a curtain for the church door, red and gold brocade.

13th June

We are moving heaven and earth to leave Palestine this year because Cliff, particularly, is so fed up with it. We have heard from the Ministry of Health, who suggested that he goes for an interview when he gets to London. Also, we have heard that his South African application has been sent on to Johannesburg. Cliff is rather keen to go there. I'm not, for obvious reasons. Still, I suppose it would be foolish, if he did get it, to turn it down, in view of the unemployment at home. There are pages in the *Architect's Journal* of advertisements from people wanting jobs.

22nd June

Have you read of the murder of Dr Arlosoroff? He was one of the Jewish leaders. A dreadful affair, political of course. It was evidently a well thought out scheme... We went to a cafe on the shore with Zelda where the murder took place. The waiter told us there were several young men playing with toy pistols, and so when the real shot was fired no-one took any notice. Charles very callously remarked that he was surprised that there were not more political murders, and that he thought the Jews were getting Palestine very easily.

25th June

We had a very jolly time yesterday. The Cooks came to tea, and Paul Pedretti, Gerald Pendred and the three little Stewarts (Jean, John and Beboes). We hired films, and so had a cinema show. Hanania had a good selection of 'Charlies' and also some of 'Stan Laurel'.

27th June

I shall be glad of a change of outlook. I'm getting tired of the Holy Land: it must be the gypsy blood in me urging me on. Cliff says he has exhausted the country. He may do another Barclay's Bank soon, in Tel Aviv, and perhaps one in Haifa, if we are still here.

You say don't go to Jo'burg. Exactly what is the alternative? We can't stay in Palestine indefinitely, and we can't afford to send the four boys to boarding school. Nor is it any joke to come home to join the unemployed. It's no good sending articles about slum areas, we can't do it philanthropically.

25th July

What shall I do with John? He is always quoting proverbs at me. The other day I had the doctor to him, as he had a temperature. The doctor said he had probably eaten too much fruit, whereupon John murmured, 'An apple a day keeps the doctor away' which really seemed rather rude! Then, yesterday, he wanted a toy pistol, and there were none in the shops. I told him to stop thinking about it as there weren't any in Jerusalem, but said John, 'Where there's a will there's a way.' These remarks are quite unanswerable. Cliff thinks that he better be a lawyer, as he always has an answer. We have decided that Timothy will probably be the architect in the family. Paul wants to go in for 'one of those ologies'. Anyway, I hope they all do something different. What shall we do with Robin? Yesterday, he was strapped in his pram, but somehow or other he got out, and Ellie found him with his head caught in the mosquito net and his legs in the air.

4th August

The patients have had a fairly bad week: scarlet fever. Cliff got a sort of rheumatism in his hands, and went very weak. He couldn't sit up without being helped. Timothy had swollen glands, and was threatened with an abscess in his ear which, thank goodness, seems to have gone away. No complications for John. Today is the first day they seem to be really better. Paul, who didn't get it, is bored to tears at Tan Tur, but until he is out of quarantine it is the only place for him. He rings up every night. Robin is well. I will try and go and see them on Monday... Jameel told me tonight that the rainwater cistern is empty, so I don't know what will happen now. We get municipal water once every five days, and it only just lasts us, with a minimum of baths. And the rotters turn it on at night, so we can't steal some for the garden when it is running!

30th August

I have got the silliest kind of scarlet fever imaginable: not a symptom, except my very thorough 'peel'; not even a sore throat. It seems absurd that I should have to stay in bed, but I suppose I must until the doctor comes again. Cliff is out now, and been to see Robin.

5th September

Sister Jenny says that Tel Aviv is packed with the German Jews, and they are paying as much as £5 a month for one room. More are expected this autumn, and every day in the papers are notices of new doctors and dentists et cetera. I heard there was a scheme for opening a big school for Jewish children who could be sent from Germany, because they are being so humiliated there. Sister Jenny is very naughty, she says 'Heil Hitler' to Robin every morning, and he waves both hands in the air.

14th September

The Ethiopian Queen – having at last decided to come – arrives on the 24th. Cliff has to show her round the church on the Tuesday. He went down yesterday with Paul to see if everything was ready. There has been a flight of steps built, from where we stood on the river bank right into the Jordan, so that the Queen can go and bathe. Apparently, according to the Abyssinians, to bathe in the Jordan makes one especially holy. Cliff, Paul, Mr Paul and several priests spent their time at the Jordan having a competition to see who could throw a stone across the river!

19th September

I am just waiting for the health people to come and disinfect the house. Im Tannas is very busy washing downstairs. She has a terrific amount to do: blankets, curtains, mosquito nets, et cetera... They have been and the house reeks of formaldehyde, so I am sitting in the garden. Fortunately, it is a very cool day. I think Paul will come back tonight, and Robin in the morning... You will be glad to know that we heard this week that the South African job has been filled. Cliff was rather dashed, but not too much, as he knew I was not very keen on going.

30th September

Cliff went to Jericho on Friday, complete with cap and gown, which he preferred to a top hat. In the train of the Ethiopian Queen were nine cars, all with the Abyssinian flag. They all went on a tour of the church and convent. Cliff thought the Queen very aloof and bad-tempered looking. She had a daughter with her, and a little son about Paul's age who was very naughty. One of the bad things he did was to turn on all the taps in the bathroom, shower and all, but probably he had never seen so many before. Cliff, Paul and I are going down tomorrow morning, when they are consecrating the church. The royal party are supposed to be going down at 4.00, but we don't intend to go there before 7.00. We are hiring a car, as the Fiat is not in good order, and the Jericho road is too steep for a sick car.

I may go with Cliff to Tel Aviv on Tuesday. I shall spend the day with Zelda. I am sending you a picture of a plan Cliff made for a Jewish Colony at Nathanyah. It is on what is supposed to be the most beautiful strip of coast in Palestine, ideal for bathing. Some people have country cottages there, and go for months in the summer, but it is a very difficult place to get at, as there is no proper road yet.

2nd October

We had a most interesting time at the Abyssinian Church. We arrived at about 6.30, in time for the most interesting part of the proceedings. The priests had been singing for some time. Royalty was in the little gallery at the back of the church and, shortly after we arrived, Cliff was taken up and presented with a gold medal. It is the Order of the Trinity, the highest order in Abyssinia. He is very bucked with it. It is quite valuable, I should imagine. Several English guests came, government people, consuls; then the Queen, the Princess and the little Prince came down. They sat in three chairs in the centre of the church, and we sat round making a sort of horseshoe. Then the procession started, very similar

Cliff and Paul at the site of the Ethiopian Church on the Jordan

King David Hotel, Jerusalem

to the one we saw on the roof of the Holy Sepulchre at Easter. The umbrellas were there and a little bell, but no tom-toms. There was plenty of incense and queer wailings and chantings. The High Priest carried what must have been something equivalent to the Ark. It must have been holy, because every time it came past (they processed round the church three times) the Queen bowed very low. Finally, it was taken to the back of the church, where there was a sort of holy of holies. The Abyssinian Church is a mixture of church and synagogue. After this, the Copts sang a little chant all about 'Suliman' and then there were three addresses read to the Queen. This was the end of the ceremony. We were then taken to the salon where there was a repast (provided by the King David) of champagne, sandwiches, cakes, ice cream and biscuits, all very nicely served and delectable. We were all then presented to the Queen, and said our goodbyes and came home. The Queen is fat and solid, with a most immobile face, but a very nice smile. I wish you could have seen the Princess's costume: it was a long white gown with gold embroidery, and on her head a white beret, much to one side with a most coquettish black lace veil to her nose. But the Minister of Finance was the funniest: he wore a very full, rather short, black cloak, beneath which was swathed a white garment with a coloured border. Under this, he wore white trousers, and on top a perfectly good English top hat!

6th October

We had an interesting evening on Tuesday. A dinner party was given by the Queen of Ethiopia at the King David Hotel. It was a lovely dinner, and with interesting guests. The heads of all the religious communities were there, Latin, Greek, Coptic, Syriac, Russian and Protestant. All the consuls and their wives, too, were there. The Chief Secretary, who is acting HE, and a few other representative English people. The Queen was very simply dressed in white silk, no jewels or headdress. The Princess, similarly dressed, was looking delightful in a full pale yellow velvet cloak. She is very good-looking, ancient Egyptian features and very small.

14th October

We thought there was going to be trouble yesterday. The Arabs announced they were going to have a procession from the mosque, pick up the Christian Arabs at the Holy Sepulchre, and march to the old Palace Hotel, which is now a Moslem building, and there have a mass meeting to protest against the immigration of the Jews in such great numbers. However, once again, they were not very successful. The police broke up the procession as it came out of the New Gate, and the meeting was not held. There were police, soldiers, armoured cars and guns all over the town. They would not have had much chance, but a wild crowd, like the Nebi Musa procession, can do quite a lot of damage if it gets really excited.

19th October

We had decided to come home at Easter if we had £1000. We can get it, on paper! But it remains to be seen what will actually happen.

21st October

Please tell father that the Ethiopians are – with the Copts – the oldest Christians in the world. They have a very ancient form of Christianity, and very primitive, but they also hold that they are the descendants of Solomon and the Queen of Sheba. Some of their customs are still Jewish: for instance, they have two separate entrances, one for men and one for women, and they do not mix in church. They have a sort of holy of holies, and in Abyssinia both Saturday and Sunday are holy days.

26th October

We had a lovely day on Sunday by the Dead Sea. It was a glorious day, and not too hot. The children spent the day in bathing costumes, and I vaselined them well so they were able to stay in the water without getting sore legs. They had great fun floating about in the water hanging on to pieces of wood. Timothy was in quite deep water when a wind got up and a wave unexpectedly knocked him over and filled his eyes and mouth with water. After that, he was quite happy to be dressed. It's beastly stuff to swallow.

There is trouble in town today. There was a demonstration in Jaffa yesterday, and it seems to have been more serious than the one here. We hear conflicting rumours, but evidently quite a number of Arabs were killed. There was trouble too in other towns, and it was said that Haifa was going to protest on the day of the opening of the harbour next week. It is all due to the number of Jews coming into the country. The Arabs think the Government should control immigration to a greater extent. It is difficult to see the end of all this.

We were discussing religion the other day, and I happened to say that Jesus Christ was a Jew. Paul was surprised, but John said, 'Well, I knew that', and Timothy (not understanding anything about it) said, 'Well, why didn't you tell me?'

31st October
Letter from Cliff to Lill

Once more, we are in the throes of riots. It is most unpleasant, but the more trouble there is the sooner we shall be home. At present, we are thoroughly fed up and suffering from very severe 'Palestineitis'. So don't pray for peace in Jerusalem if you want us home next year! I am a Special again, in uniform, with a gun and fifty rounds. I haven't done much yet, and don't intend to do much either. I have decided to defend my family, not Jews: last time was enough. Although the tension is at breaking point, it looks as if the whole business will blow over providing Thursday – Balfour Declaration Day – passes without demonstrations. It's all very nerve-racking and thoroughly unpleasant. Apart from the general unrest, we are all well and fit. Robin, in particular, is full of beans: you would love him, he's such a very blue-eyed boy. Paul, John and Tigger (Timothy now) are at school. John takes his first music examination – Trinity College – before Christmas. Paul still does Latin. Eunice is helping me to do 'quantities' for a new school, and I am doing Bishop Gobat's. I've got a most beautiful study in this house, about 18 by 10 feet, and with a double vault. This part of our lives is all that could be desired.

1st November

It must have been very disappointing for all the people that the opening (of Barclay's Bank) had to be given up. There was to be a great luncheon with speeches, and a firework display at night. Several people came from England especially for it, and all that took place was a very quiet opening by the HE, with no ceremony. Of course the Arabs could not have attended, and to have it with English and Jews would not have been wise, to say the least of it. We have not seen anything of the disturbances here in the German Colony, but Cliff says the atmosphere in the town is most unpleasant, groups of Arabs – who are all on strike – standing about, police in tin hats and armoured cars. They called Cliff up as a Special, but he refused to go out at night, so he was given the necessary uniform and told he would be called in the day-time if wanted. We have heard nothing since. I think it was only a precautionary measure. They want to avoid, if possible, calling out the army. We hope that the worst is over, but it is Balfour Day tomorrow and then another Friday. The strike is supposed to be on until Saturday, which makes a week. There is one shop in the colony always open, but his supply of vegetables gets less and less. I think what has upset them this time is that the leaders have been put in Acre prison, all except old Moussa Kasim Pasha, who is over eighty. He was in the row at Jaffa, and had to be rescued by the police as he was being so knocked about.

6th November

We hear today that Professor Abercrombie is coming out in December, so Cliff will be working with him on the Haifa plan. It will be nice to see him again, he is very cheerful.

10th November

Yesterday, Cliff and I escaped from the family of five, did a little shopping and had coffee in the Vienna cafe, where we saw lots of Jewish friends and, incidentally, bought Flanders poppies. We then went to the pictures, and afterwards to the German Restaurant for supper. There, we met Pringle and Parker, who brought us home and stayed for a while. I had not seen them for ages;

they always talk of Elizabeth and remember their visit to her. All our disturbances are over for the time being. I believe the Arabs are very bitter and have got hold of all sorts of false tales. I see the English papers talk of anti-Jewish riots. This was not so, it was definitely anti-government this time. It was not serious enough for us to suffer any inconvenience. The Arabs don't hang together. They will sell land to the Jews, in spite of it all, so what can you expect?

19th November

What might have led to a raid on Jews was stopped by a native policeman. On Saturday, a big crowd came out of the mosque – chiefly Hebronites, I believe – and tried to burn down the Jewish quarter. There was one British policeman and one Arab there. The British policeman stood with his rifle across the street trying to stop the mob. Of course he was overpowered, but was just able to shout 'Fire' to the Arab before he was knocked down. Fortunately, the Arab was quick and plucky: he fired into the crowd, which was so great that he killed five and wounded about 15. And that was the end of that. The Arabs still sound very threatening, and will blow up at any increase of immigration of Jews. And, of course, if it is curtailed in any way, the Jews curse us like blazes. We can't do anything right. I think it is a pity we don't pack up and leave this unholy land. There is a curse on this country.

23rd November

We went to a dinner party on Thursday to meet Mr and Mrs Mendelsohn. You may not know him: he is, or was, the most famous German architect of today. He did a lot of the new German work in Berlin. However, being a Jew, he was told to go. He had built himself a beautiful house, it must have been terrible to leave it. Mrs Mendelsohn is simply beautiful, and I wish you could have seen her dress. It must have been the kind you wore in your youth, velvet with a tight bodice with little buttons all round the front and some lovely old lace round the neck which was pinned with an old brooch. She wore here hair parted down the middle and brushed straight down, with a knob at the back; her features are so perfect it suited her that way. She is of Spanish Jewish stock. They are both terribly sad at having to leave, and do not know where to go.

The pictures you sent were interesting, as the architect was the Erich Mendelsohn we met last week, and we also met Mr Schocken, for whom the big store was built. Mendelsohn is building him a house in Jerusalem.

28th November

You ask about the use of the word Ethiopian. I had it explained to me by the Egyptian Consul, who was sitting by me at dinner. Ethiopian is correct, and always used by the Ethiopians themselves.

Nathanyah is an orange-growing colony. I believe it is going to be a very popular place. The price of land is going up tremendously there. So it is here in Haifa of course. We went down the new 'frontal' road yesterday, it is to be named 'Kingsway'. With proper control of buildings, it should be a very fine street. It is actually on the reclaimed areas and so, at the moment, has all the old seafront of Haifa along one side, and a more dilapidated collection of buildings would be hard to imagine. There should be a tremendous amount of building going on soon, but I think Cliff would have to get many large and interesting jobs to compensate for living in Haifa.

2nd December

We got back from Haifa on Saturday, and found all the children well and happy. Our day at El Hamme, the hot springs, was most entertaining. We had to go to Tiberias, then round the south end of the Sea of Galilee, across the Jordan and up the Yarmuk Valley. We went along the road that was by the old Turkish railway, the one Lawrence blew up in several places during the war. El Hamme is a sort of no-man's-land, or what Suliman Bey calls his own country, because Transjordan is south of the river and Syria is north of the railway, and El Hamme is in between. We had a wonderful bathe in what is known as the champagne bath. It is a fairly large bath, big enough to swim in, and with a natural pebbly floor. The water is bubbling up through the floor all the time, and is quite hot, it's lovely. Some of the springs are particularly good for boils and skin diseases. In the season (spring) the valley is full of Syrians, Palestinians, Egyptians and Bedouins et cetera, all bathing and living in tents. The whole valley smells of eggs, not necessarily bad ones, but certainly eggs: one gets used to it after a little while. We had lunch there with Suliman Bey and a guest, the second Chief of the Druse rebels in the rebellion against the French in 1925(?) He is condemned to death if he re-enters Syria, and Suliman Bey was very worried because the road passes through Syria. However, the Druse said he didn't mind. He was a very good-looking gentlemanly Arab with a very kind face and a red beard.

The Professor arrives on the eleventh (Abercrombie). Cliff is going to Haifa to meet him. It will be nice to have him for Christmas... I forgot to tell you that El Hamme has remains of Roman buildings, baths and an amphitheatre, and the mosaic floor of a synagogue.

(No date)

Cliff is very busy working for the Professor. They have got a room in the YMCA to do the Haifa plans, so they can be quiet and undisturbed; it is quite a good job for Cliff. He has also definitely got the Tel Aviv Barclay's Bank, which has to be started at once, so things don't look too hopeless... I will get you the photographs of Robin: he is an unruly baby, but very clever.

27th December

We had a jolly Christmas party and the prettiest tree we have ever had. Robin has learnt to blow a trumpet, and blows it loud and long. He can't walk alone yet. He loves parties and crowds and noise and crackers et cetera. Cliff and the Professor took Christmas day off, but are working hard all the rest of the time.

15

1934

T here is a switch in attention this year from Jerusalem to Haifa. Haifa was, with Tel Aviv, one of the fast-growing towns on the coast, with its own harbour works and foreshore reclamation. Professor Abercrombie was involved with the plans, and the High Commissioner, Sir Arthur Wauchope, was anxious that Cliff should continue with this and other buildings in Haifa. A technical college, a power station and a Barclay's Bank were three that were built. Cliff opened an office in Haifa, and an architect out from England joined him. This was Pearce Hubbard, a tall and flamboyant character who married Frances Bruce, a sculptress.

The other arrival was Hilda, a German who was to be a nurse for Robin, and was eventually to return to England with the family and stay until the beginning of the war. The return was now the subject of exchanges with Elizabeth and others over schools. Eunice and Cliff were definitely against boarding schools, so St Pauls, in London, was one considered. Paul and I eventually went there.

The work in Haifa reflected the consolidation of the Jewish community in Palestine. What had begun as a relatively small-scale village and agricultural development had now become some very heavy investment in Tel Aviv, Haifa, Nathanyah and other towns. There was no looking back, as immigration and capital increased rapidly, and it must have been clear that troubles with the Arab community would grow. The work atmosphere for Cliff was also different. In Jerusalem, at the beginning of the Mandate, there had been much that was historical and archaeological. Now, with the growth of the coastal towns, modern architecture, uninfluenced by tradition, was the rule, and it can be seen in Cliff's work. Palestine was changing from an ancient country to a modern one.

5th January

Cliff and the Prof. had the usual rush finishing the plan. I was called in at the end to draw trees. Tree-planted boulevards by the mile, I think I drew hundreds, no thousands. It is an enormous stretch of land between Haifa and Acre, Jewish property, to be a second Tel Aviv I suppose, but a more industrial one. They went up to Haifa yesterday for the final meeting, and the Professor is on his way home.

27th January

Charles Sassoon rang up: he had come to spend a night at the King David Hotel, and it was full. Not a single bedroom, over 400 guests, so he asked if he could stay with us. He had come to see Sir Montague and Lady Burton: you probably know the shops. Anyway, he is a Jew – a millionaire – and comes from Yorkshire. They live in Harrogate. We went and met them after dinner, a tiny little man and a very large wife, both quite pleasant. They were on the *Empress of Britain* and going round the world.

31st January

We are expecting a visitor next week, an old student of Liverpool who won the Prix de Rome and quarrelled with the authorities because he wanted to do his thesis on Modern Architecture and they wouldn't let him. So he threw up his 'Prix' and is coming here via Constantinople. He asked Cliff to give him a job, 'enough money to keep body and soul together'. The Prof. and Lazarus both say he is very nice: his name is Pearce Hubbard.

We have with us the Prix de Rome scholar I told you about: he is very nice indeed, very enthusiastic and cheerful, and thrilled with Jerusalem. He wants to get a room to live in the old city. He has done some really beautiful water colour sketches; and he is 6'3"! He is staying with us until he finds a room.

We dined at Government House on Friday. It was quite a small party: the English Consul and his wife from Damascus, who were staying there, a lady who was acting as hostess (HE Sir Arthur Wauchope is a bachelor), the private secretary, the ADC[5] and another man. The ADC took me in to dinner but I sat by HE. He is quite nice to talk to. Afterwards, he had a very long conversation with Cliff about taking over some Government architectural work, but more of this later when it is settled. Anyway, he sent Cliff a very nice appreciative letter later about it. The outcome of all this will probably decide our plans for the next two years. Cliff can't afford to throw up a really good chance, as we have scarcely enough to risk coming home just yet without a job.

13th February

I'm in Haifa again. Lulu is in charge at home, and also our guest, Mr Hubbard, a very accommodating young man, who can be left at will and makes himself at home. Cliff is busy seeing about the new Barclay's Bank. Did I tell you he was doing a Haifa as well as a Tel Aviv one? And the Haifa Branch is really large, a six storey building, I believe. Also, Cliff has been given a job by the Government, a Trade School at Haifa, and been promised more. This is rather a smack in the eyes for Harrison and there are terrible rows going on at PWD[2] but Cliff has HE[4] and the Chief Secretary backing him up. The trouble is that Public Works don't get on with a job. The Post Office had been going for five years, and they haven't

Family at Jaffa

At the German Hospice, Haifa

started building. It's rather exciting, as Cliff might get a rather important building out of it. On all this, too, depends whether we come home or not. The joke was that HE offered Cliff the Post Office. But Cliff refused it, as PWD have already got a certain amount done. It is rather rough on Harrison, as he is supposed to do all Government buildings, but there is stacks to do, and Harrison is an artist and a dreamer. Of course the result is that we simply don't know what to do.

Haifa

Model of Kingsway, Haifa

27th February
To Elizabeth

Continue sending prospectuses by all means but, I warn you, the more I read, the more completely am I put off boarding schools. Cliff is off anyway. I don't know anything about Choir Schools, naturally, but Mrs Cooke does, and she says the boys are just exploited to get a good choir. Mr Piersenne, the organist here at St George's, was from one. He was an utter failure, and has gone back to England. It makes one think. I wrote for Winnie's opinion, and had her reply just after yours. She thinks boarding schools only if one can afford the very best. Jo thinks as I do, the first break from home should be at 17 or 18. However, we dodder along and don't worry. I doubt if we'll be able to come in July. Now Barclay's have bought their two sites, Tel Aviv and Haifa, Cliff says he can't leave until he has prepared all plans, working drawings, specifications, quantities, and got the contract signed. I think this will take months so I'm not planning anything.

We found Hubbard a room in the old city, with a roof where he can paint. It is near the Haram, and he has a lovely view of the Dome of the Rock. Lazarus thinks it disgraceful: he rents a room in a Moslem house for a pound a month then feeds in the Jewish Workers' restaurant for 5 or 3 piastres a meal. We promised him a hot bath and a beef steak once a week. He came on Sunday, and did full justice to the steak but, like you, sees no necessity for washing in Palestine, and refused the bath.

Cliff is finding Hubbard very jolly to have in the office. He is a very charming and cheerful young man, most unconventional, goes about in a sweater and patched trousers. When John remarked that he didn't like wearing patched trousers he said, 'Oh John, what at snob'. His father was one of the designers of the R 101[6]. Cliff, at the moment, is busy on: (1) Tel Aviv bank; (2) cinema for Nathanyah; (3) block of flats and shops; (4) worker's settlement, Haifa Bay; (5) block of classrooms for Ramallah School.

So he is busy. He took his lunch every day this week. He is to share it today with Hubbard, Hubbard's contribution being a bottle of Richon wine and about eight oranges, tied up in a spotted handkerchief.

28th February

Cliff thinks you will be interested to read the letter he got from the High Commissioner (*Sir Arthur Wauchope*). When he asked some authority in what way he should reply, they said they had never heard of anyone receiving a private letter from a High Commissioner before! Anyway HE is obviously going to give him as much work as possible.

Cliff found Paul smoking behind the sofa. He said, 'If I had done that, my father would have whipped me'. Paul replied 'Yes, but your father was so old-fashioned, wasn't he?' Cliff asked John yesterday if he thought I was pretty. John, after much thought, replied, 'Three-quarters pretty and one quarter ugly'.

20th March
To Elizabeth

I wish you could see our garden. 'Our' rock garden is green all over, the Mesem is luxuriant... I think you have the idea that what prevents us sending Paul home is the expense. This is not so. If we were both decided he ought to go, we would produce the money. No, Cliff definitely does not approve, and I don't think I do. Hubbard thinks we are mad to send them to England. He says he is just beginning to be natural again after his schooling. He was at Bedford, a day boy. I wrote to Winnie to ask what she and Jo thought, and the answer was the same, avoid boarding school at all costs. I met, the other day, a very charming old lady, the mother of Mr Thornton-Dewsbury, the new Head of St George's, and she agreed, too, which is not what I would have expected.

A week today, we hope to go to Nathanyah for ten days holiday by the sea. It is the Jewish Colony that Cliff made a plan for. There is a quite up-to-date hotel there. The only drawback is that it will be Passover, and we shall get no bread, only matsos. However, I've no doubt the children will enjoy being able to eat biscuits for every meal. Cliff's new jobs, together with having Hubbard to work with and giving up the Government part of his work, seem to have cured him of what he called his 'Palestineitis'. I'm very glad. There's no doubt the work is interesting. The man who got the job Cliff applied for – Town Planning Inspector for the Ministry of Health – was mentioned in the *Manchester Guardian* as having been sent from London to Salford to decide whether a house could be turned into a shop! It gave Cliff quite a pain to think he might have been the man. When you think of the things he has to do here... He has been offered the control of buildings on the new wide street called Kingsway, which runs along the back of the reclaimed area at Haifa. One side is unbuilt-upon, and the other side will be rebuilt, so it's a clear field and they want to make a good thing out of it.

22nd March

You asked who is Lazarus? He is a Jewish boy, Jack Lazarus from Middlesborough, who was at Liverpool the same time as Hubbard and came out here over a year ago, when Cliff gave him a job in the office. He is very nice, quiet and steady. But not brilliant like Hubbard. We, too, thought about having Hubbard to stay in the office. He seems to be quite keen. He loves this part of the world. Cliff has just been to Tiberias to see one of his buildings there, an annex to the Scottish Hospital. I have not seen the Princess Royal, although she has been about the town a lot. Cliff saw Lord Lascelles (Harewood, sorry) at a Masonic meeting. He was asked to go, otherwise he doesn't go to these meetings very much: he's rather bored with them.

11th April
To Elizabeth
Nathanyah

I am sitting on the shore in a bathing costume. We are enjoying this holiday. The coast is different from any other in Palestine. We walk from our hotel over sandhills which remind me of Birkdale. Then we clamber down a steep path to the shore, quite a narrow strip of shore with high cliffs at the back, lovely for the children to climb. Ellie takes Robin back at eleven, and he has his sleep and lunch and comes back at about three. He loves to sit on the sand and play, but is rather afraid of the waves. It is the first time he has seen the sea. Nathanyah is a very small colony, surrounded by orange groves. Last night, there was an east wind which blew the scent of the orange blossom right over us. It was beautiful.

21st April
To Elizabeth

His appointment (Cliff's) as an extra Government architect has been approved, so he can get on with the Technical College and, this week, HE definitely offered him the new street Kingsway in Haifa, to design the frontage and control all buildings that go up. Last week, he had an odd collection of jobs offered: two water towers, Haifa Power Station for Rutenburg (who apparently is very hard to please: he has tried about ten Jewish architects) and a layout for a Bahai Garden. Do you remember the Bahais? He has moved his office to the building at the back of the YMCA. It is the old YM drawing office, where Mr Adamson used to be, a lovely cool, quiet place.

Do you remember the bandit Abu Jilda? The police have just caught him. He was given away by his cousin. The Arabs have turned him into a hero. But I expect he will be hanged. Pringle and Parker came to see us the other night to say goodbye. They have been sent to South Africa to study, and bring back a special kind of police dog which has been bred there. The English bloodhound is no good here, it cannot stand the climate.

18th May

Cliff and I dined with Hubbard one evening in his tiny room in the Convent of the Cross. It's a terribly old monastery – Greek – and most romantic inside. He has a primus stove, so we fried sausages and tomatoes and ate native bread and olives. We all sat on the bed afterwards as he has only stools. We had to leave fairly early, as the gateman was waiting to let us out. Usually the door is locked at eight o'clock.

30th May

We're in Haifa again. I came up with Cliff on Monday morning. He has had stacks of things to do here and lots of people to see, and Rutenburg is what Cliff calls a Mussolini. I met the great man yesterday (Rutenburg, not Mussolini). Yesterday we went to see a worker's settlement on Haifa Bay lands. Rows and rows of little houses all on the sand. But they are trying hard, and making some really nice gardens. I was given a huge bouquet of flowers and some strawberries fresh from the gardens to eat. Cliff had to go round the land, as he is doing a scheme for it. So I stayed in one of the houses and talked, with difficulty, to a Lithuanian Jew who has recently come to Palestine. Later we went up Mount Carmel, as Cliff had to see Father Lamb of the Carmelite Monastery.

6th June

Cliff has finally decided to have Hubbard as a junior partner, and now he is looking for some other Englishman who can do the more constructional part. Then he will open an office in Haifa and have the third man there.

27th June

I sacked Jameel yesterday. He is supposed to be in charge of the house when we are away, and not leave it, and I found he had been out every night, and so today is going. I've had him six years!

5th July

At last the nurse – Hilda (really Hildegarde) – has arrived, and she seems just what I want. Plain, solid and thoroughly dependable. Robin likes her because she is quiet and soft-voiced. Her sister, Frieda, is looking after a little girl of sixteen months, so they all go out together in the afternoons. Paul and John have gone off very thrilled this afternoon. They are playing a cricket match against Bishop Gobat's school (little Arab boys). It seems absurd, they are all so small. Anyway, Cliff has bought them a real cricket bat.

You would laugh at my two servants. Two little Arab boys, both about the same size and about thirteen years old. They work like little Trojans, and are both so anxious to stay (because they are both on trial) that they simply fall over themselves in their eagerness to help. They are called Da'oud (David) and Diab, and both come from the same village, in fact they are cousins. I am teaching Diab to cook, and he shows great aptitude. He has been working for a German lady for one and a half years, so knows more than the other one. I hope they will prove successful, because they are nice little boys, and besides I am saving money, as they only get £1.10 a month each. They neither of them speak English, so I shall learn a little more Arabic.

160

The house in the German Colony

A coal delivery camel; the house in the German Colony

17th July

Cliff doesn't have the energy for letter-writing, there is so much to be done. Hubbard is good but spasmodic, and at the moment he is distracted by a girl who has come to see him from Rome. A Rome Scholar, a sculptress called Frances Bruce. She is awfully nice. Reminds me a little of Winnie. Her father is a great educationalist, and knows Toynbee well. Hubbard wants to marry her, but she seems to be rather afraid of getting married at the moment. However, I hope she will change her mind, as I think they would be well suited. She leaves for England next week. We all went on a jolly picnic to the Hebron oaks on Saturday.

Paul, John, Timothy and Robin; the house in the German Colony

25th July

We have cricket enthusiasts ringing up or coming to hear the wireless; one particular neighbour calls, with his wife, about seven to hear the results of the Test Matches... My two small servants are too much for me. They don't remember what they are told, and they do play, and often the play turns into a fight, and perhaps one weeps. Small Arab boys weep easily. I am going to interview a German girl tomorrow, a friend of Hilda's who might come as a cook.

We set off on Friday with a brand new car, an American Auburn saloon, very pale fawn, which is a good colour for this country because it doesn't show the dust. Yesterday, we went to Athlit for the day, a lovely place. Antiquities are working on the old crusader castle and have cleared out two rooms, one they think was a banqueting hall: it is beautifully vaulted. The castle is on a marvellous site, built on rocks right on the sea edge. The crusaders must have been as much craftsmen as soldiers. Cliff met a friend: a Mr Waddington, of Antiquities, he is living in a bungalow with his very young wife, a dog, six newly born puppies, several cats and a tame hawk. It is a heavenly spot to live, but there always seems to be a drawback, Mrs Waddington has just had malaria. Robin enjoyed his day on the shore, but was terribly tired afterwards, and we had to throw him into bed when we got home. Paul and John had a lovely time with the cubs. There were twelve cubs and three brownies. Miss Miller and Akela looked exhausted when we went to visit them. Some of the little boys were very small. One of the youngest was Paul Spicer, son of the Chief of Police. Miss Miller said, on the day, 'Well, Paul, will you be glad to see your mother?' He replied, 'I'll be glad to see my tortoise'… Timothy's latest: he was walking behind Cliff and me on the shore and suddenly remarked, 'Are you two married yet!'

21st August

Our romantic bandit Adu Jilda was hanged this morning, to the great regrets of the Arabs. Very strangely, the police officer who was to have hanged him died of a heart failure in his sleep last night. I am afraid the Arabs will say it was the visitation of Allah… The house is full of cricket. I've never heard or known so much about it before. The children are so excited about this Test Match.

28th August

Frances, Hubbard's fiancee, has left us and gone to England via Rome. She is coming back sometime to get married. Hubbard has got a house in Ain Karim; he has a Russian woman to come to clean and cook for him.

7th September

You ask if Hilda speaks English. Yes, very well. She has been to England. Robin gets mixed with German and sometimes, in answer to a question, says, 'No, no, no, nein'. Did I tell you that Hilda listened to Hitler on the wireless for two hours one night?

Cliff is tremendously busy on the design for the Kingsway, a terrific problem, a whole street with a station square and an entrance to the harbour. There is a Mr Hervey here, a specialist in restoring old buildings. He was got out to restore the Holy Sepulchre dome, then asked to do the roof of the Nativity church in Bethlehem. Apparently, he dug down first to see if the foundations of the columns were firm, and discovered an old marble floor. Being something of an archaeologist, he dug further, and came to the original mosaics. Quite a lot of the nave is complete, and probably the aisles are there too. Mr Hervey's proposal is to restore the original floor on a firm foundation. I hope the Government will do it. Amazing to think it has been there all these years undiscovered.

6th October

This will not be a very long letter, as I am putting in all my spare time at the office. The Kingsway plans are to be ready on Monday, and Cliff has to take them to Haifa on Tuesday. There are five big sheets and three perspectives and a report, so you can guess it is rather a rush at the end. I was at the office all yesterday afternoon and am going again today.

12th October

Cliff finished the drawings in time, and they were approved right away by Mr Pudsey (of PWD), then he and Pearce (Hubbard) took them to the meeting in

Haifa, and everyone was very pleased with them so it is all very satisfactory.

The children all went to the police sports on Thursday. Hilda took them, and Robin quite enjoyed himself; he liked the horses jumping. The camels danced round the maypole...

19th October
The Herfords are back from their leave (in case you have forgotten, Herford was the old boy from Alan Taylor's school who come here from Baghdad). Cliff is so wishing that Herford was with him instead of at the municipality, but he got the job before Cliff's rush of work came along. We took them house hunting yesterday. They are both very nice. Both from Manchester. Herford lapses into broad Lancashire on occasions: I think it makes him feel at home.

23rd October
Cliff has to go to Amman, in Transjordan, next week. They want a town plan. I would love to go, but it is the day my new cook arrives.

14th November
To Elizabeth
Haifa
Do you remember finding a sheltered spot in the Carmel Convent garden, and sitting there in the sun and looking at the bay? I am there at the moment. Haifa is growing tremendously, and at night from the new panorama road the lights look marvellous. The Rutenburg power station is lit up all over, as they are working on it day and night, in three eight-hour shifts; it is right on the shore, and will look most conspicuous from the sea. It is amazingly clear today, I can see Herman and the Lebanon.

Cliff is at a town planning meeting this morning, getting the big plan passed that he and the Professor worked on last Christmas. It is for the Haifa Bay lands but, oh dear, what quarrelsome people they are. So many parties: there are the Labour group, the Communist group, the new German group, et cetera, and they won't mix.

27th December
We have had a quiet(?) Christmas. That is no visitors, except Pearce, who was here all the time, and Miss Graves (sister of Charles Graves) who came to tea. We had lots of callers, and Zelda and Charles blew in on Christmas afternoon.

Dinner was a riotous affair, with crackers and a pudding with charms in. Pearce got the bachelor's button, which was rather sad as Frances is coming out to marry him next month. However, the matter was put right last night when we ate up the pudding and he unexpectedly got the ring.

31st December

The party was a great success. I had Timothy's friends, seven small boys, in a separate room, as the others were too riotous. They ended up with a fight with streamers and carnival balls. Cliff had Pearce to help him, and Thomas Concannon came in the middle, and had five boys on top of him all at once. You should have seen the room when it was over. We had a home cinema for a lot of the time, which kept them quiet.

16

1935

By April this year, Eunice and Cliff finally made plans to return to England. In August came the departure, and the end of thirteen years in Palestine, half the period of the Mandate. In 1936, an Arab rebellion broke out in protest against the rate of Jewish immigration, and then came the war and the Jewish fight for the State of Israel.

So the family had lived through the most interesting and rewarding time of the Mandate, seeing Jerusalem and much of Palestine as it had been after centuries of Ottoman rule, an ancient city entering a modern world. Jerusalem has now turned from a relatively small and backward Arabic town to an Israeli metropolis of over half a million.

19th January
To Elizabeth

Cliff is worried to death to know what is best to do. He has been offered a big job, and it seems absurd to turn it down. I don't think he will ever not have any work here. It is a problem isn't it? Paul is definitely asking to go home to school. Of course, the idea of coming out here in summer on the school children's boat thrills him to the core. We must decide soon. Thomas Concannon is here for the weekend, so the matter will be discussed at great length, I am sure. Winnie wants to come in the summer.

We don't see many people these days. I said this to Zelda, and she gave me a lecture on becoming middle-aged. Pearce and Frances are being married on Sunday at St. George's, a very quiet wedding. Young Mr McInnes is marrying them.

13th April

Robin is getting better but very slowly (*Robin had been quite ill in hospital, but there is no letter about it*).

Cliff is working at top speed to get finished by June. It is going to be a struggle; I don't know how he keeps going. He has had only one holiday in the last four years, and this country is not an easy one to work in. Did I tell you that he has got the station in Haifa to do? My missionary is going to stay until I leave: she says she feels it her duty. She thinks she is of help to me, with little Robin ill. She doesn't mind how much beef tea and special puddings she has to make. She is so willing and good-tempered, I am lucky to find her just at this time.

30th April

Cliff and I have been evolving wonderful plans in the last few months… I will explain. Firstly, we are giving up our house here and going to have a home in England. We don't want to put the boys into boarding school and secondly, Cliff is very anxious to open an office in London, so that if the building here suddenly gives out, he will have a foot in at home. We never intended to live here for ever. It seems sensible to do the moving gradually, and Cliff must do all the work he has on hand. He will probably have to come back here for a month or two, bringing, I hope, an able assistant. I have already sold most of the furniture, and we leave the house in June. Elizabeth can send along all ideas as to where we should live.

Robin improves: he gained only three ounces last week, but we are having a spell of desert wind and very hot weather so we none of us feel like eating much. I'm hectic with: (1) selling furniture; (2) making John a Mikado suit; (3) making a suit for Robin for a Jubilee party at Government House; (4)) working in the office; (5) thinking about packing. The Dramatic Society is doing the Mikado, and they have asked John to be the little boy who runs behind Koko and holds the snickersnee. He is very excited. It means two very late nights for him and a matinee, but I couldn't refuse, for he is so thrilled about it.

Cliff has been very busy (in Haifa). He is planning a large piece of land at the foot of Carmel which belongs to an Arab who wants to develop it. He has a school there too, a boys' boarding school. There are all sorts of jobs in the office, Haifa is booming. They are going to enlarge the harbour already.

8th May

Cliff got all the things off for his M.Arch. this morning, so I feel I can breathe a little.

We had quite a lively Jubilee Day. We saw the gathering of the procession in the morning: soldiers, sailors (from the Dispatch at Haifa), Air Force, a lovely Transjordanian Frontier Force on wonderful horses (much the most striking party), armoured cars et cetera and aeroplanes flying in formation overhead. We ran up to town and saw the procession again, and ate ice cream! In the afternoon we went to the party at Government House. The most exciting part of this was donkeys and camels to ride in the garden. Paul says he went on a camel five times. After that we went to the barracks for a marvellous firework display, followed by a ride round the town to see the lights. Cliff has got a Jubilee medal.

18th May
To Elizabeth
I am so excited at the idea of having a home in England. Cliff has cheered up wonderfully since we made up our minds.

6th July
Well, things seem to be looking a little brighter. Firstly, Robin is much better. Secondly, the Trade School site is not going to be changed. The Jewish National Fund have given in – they say for Cliff's sake – so the contract will be signed within three weeks. Meanwhile, the bank and other things should settle themselves. We are now looking up boats sailing the beginning of August.

7th July
I expect we shall come by *Orsova*, Orient Line, leaving on the 17th August and arriving in London. Blast!! The only consolation I can see is that the *Orsova* calls at Naples, Toulon and Gibraltar, and so will be a new route.

13th July
Did I tell you that we had Harry Cressal here? The Cressals' English nurse was killed in a motor accident. They have had her for four years – such a very nice girl – so we have got Harry for a week. If he wants to stay I shall keep him: he is no trouble, and amuses John, they are both cricket fiends.

25th July
Cliff has just received a letter from Budden, congratulating him on getting the M.Arch. He is the first student to get it by examination (that is by work he has done).

Extraordinary things are happening. The German Consul here has got the sack, presumably because his wife had a Jewish grandmother, so it says in the paper today. It will be a blow to them, and they were popular here, and nice people.

31st July
Once more, we have had a very strenuous week. We have moved half the office furniture from Jerusalem to Haifa, and finally moved out of our home. We sent off all our packages to England (Oh! what forms to be filled in) settled our passports and, finally, Cliff has signed three big contracts. There is room for us on the City boat sailing on the 13th due in England on the 25th. If it should dock at Plymouth, we shall try to get on the *Orsova*, sailing on the 17th.

Robin continues to improve, eats well and sleeps well. Hamd'ull'allah.

The family with Eunice's mother and father at their home in Birkdale

Epilogue

The family settled in London from 1935 to 1939, living at 44 The Green, Richmond, and Cliff opened an office in central London, returning to Haifa for one period of about six months. In 1939, before the war, he went with Eunice, Timothy and Robin to Ceylon for a six-month period to prepare a town plan for Colombo. The war came when they were still out there, and Paul and I, in England, were evacuated with the rest of St Pauls, our school. In June 1940, we left England in the last wartime ship full of children sailing to parents in India and Ceylon, and eventually joined the family in Colombo. A spell in Cape Town followed between 1940 and 1942, and then a return to Ceylon. Paul and I joined up from Ceylon and Cliff, Eunice, Timothy and Robin went to Gibraltar, where Cliff prepared a plan for the Rock. At the end of the war, Cliff became the first Chief Architect for Stevenage new town. His final post was as Professor of Town and Country Planning at the University of Manchester, where he died in 1960.

Eunice died in 1992, aged 92. The stay in Jerusalem was probably the most significant period of her life, and perhaps her favourite subject of conversation!

The children are still pursuing their various careers and interests, Paul became a plant pathologist, and worked abroad a great deal; I became a town planner and landscape architect; Timothy, a painter and Robin a geneticist and cell biologist, now an FRS. The many grandchildren gave Eunice endless interest and she returned it to them, for she was a fascinating person with a unique outlook on life. The letters explain why.

Notes on the text

1 *A Personal History*, A.J.P. Taylor, Hamish Hamilton, 1983

2 PWD: Public Works Department

3 *Orientations*, by Sir Ronald Storrs, Ivor Nicholson and and Watson, 1937

4 HE: His Excellency, form of address for a High Commissioner or Ambassador

5 ADC: Aide de Camp, main assistant to a senior official or officer

6 R101: pioneering British airship

Short bibliography

David Bomberg in Palestine 1923-1927, The Israel Museum of Jerusalem, 1983

Bentwich, Norman, *England in Palestine*, London, 1932

Bahat, Dan, *The Illustrated Atlas of Jerusalem*, Simon and Schuster, 1990

Keith-Roach, Edward, *Pasha of Jerusalem*, The Radcliffe Press, 1994

Luke, Sir Harry and Keith-Roach, Edward, *The Handbook of Palestine and Transjordan*, Macmillan, 1934

Murphy-O'Connor, Jerome, *The Holy Land, An Archaeological Guide*, Oxford University Press, 1992

Rose, John Melkon, *Armenians in Jerusalem*, The Radcliffe Press, 1993

Samuel, Viscount, *Memoirs of the Rt Hon. Viscount Samuel*, Cresset Press, 1945

Samuel, Edwin, *A Lifetime in Jerusalem*, 1970

Storrs, Sir Ronald, *Orientations*, Ivor Nicholson and Watson, 1937

Index

Abercrombie, Prof. 1, 109, 119, 151

Abu Jilda (bandit) 159, 163

Abyssinian (Ethiopian) Church 132, 138, 145-147

Acre 78

Ain Farah 46, 69

Ain Kareem 46, 98

air flights 128, 130, 142

Aksa Mosque 90

Alieh 29

Allenby, Lord 3, 9, 72

American Colony 9, 11 134

Amman 114
    town plan 164

Arab Executive 81

Archaeology, School of 6, 9

Architects, fancy dress dance 81, 82

Architectural Society 31, 34

Arlosoroff, Dr 143

Ashbee, C.R. 5, 6, 11

Askalon 6, 9, 13, 15

Athlit 121, 162

Baalbec 29

Balfour, Arthur 52, 53
    Declaration 4

Barclays banks 64, 131, 143, 149, 151

Bedouin 15, 85, 141

Beirout, church at 75, 99, 100

Ben Dor 52, 55, 56, 63, 81, 87, 105, 107, 114

Beni Sakhr (tribe) 103

Bentwich, Norman 10

Bethlehem 23, 34, 112, 124, 141

Bible Society building 61, 70, 74, 75, 78

Blackwell, Polly and Joshua 1

Bomberg, Alice and David 18, 24, 39, 40, 46, 59, 61, 62, 74, 78, 83

Bristol Gardens 11

British Cemetery 12

British Government Commission 96, 124

Bruce, Frances 153, 161, 164, 166

Butt, Clara 131

Capernaum 60

Chaikin, family 61

Chancellor, Sir John 94

children of Eunice, births
    John 51
    Paul 21
    Robin 135
    Timothy 99

christenings 26, 54, 55, 123

cinema 77

Citadel 6, 23, 30, 77

clock tower 25, 34, 49

Cosen, Miss 72, 73, 104, 107, 110

Damascus 29

Danziger, Dr 100

d'Aubigny, Philip, tomb of 57, 58

Dead Sea 65, 130, 148

Deedes, Mrs and Sir William 13

Dome of the Rock 5, 8

Earthquakes 74, 83

Einstein, Albert 19

Electricity installation 80, 99

El Hamme hot springs 151

Ellie (home help) 131, 134

Elijah, feast of 27

Elizabeth (Eunice's sister)
    visits 18, 64, 130, 132
    letters from 26-31 66-69, 89-91,
    140-142

Faud, King 90

Feisal, King 90

Galilee 59, 60

Garstang, Prof. and Mrs 6, 9, 12, 15,
93, 94

Gaza 86, 126

Geddes, Patrick 4

Gerash 114

German Colony 39, 43, 138, 142

German Hospices
    Galilee 59, 84-85
    Haifa 71, 76, 94
    Jerusalem 43

Gethsemane 14

Gildersome 52, 94

Haifa 28, 76, 120, 128, 153, 164
    Kingsway 151 163

Harmat 56, 107

Harrison, Austen 27, 155

Hebron 38, 47

Herford 33, 164

Herod, King 91

Hervey, Mr 163

Home, Mr and Mrs 13-15

Hilda (Shwarz) 153, 160

Holliday, Mr and Mrs (Cliff's parents)
119, 120

Hollinshead, Eleanor 57, 64

Holy Sepulchre 5, 6, 43
    Calvary Chapel 111
    Holy Fire 36, 44
    Moslem guard 28

Hospital 21, 22

Houses
    Beit Gebshi 9
    Beit Musa 26
    Beit Syriac 36, 41
    Beit Nassar 112
    German Colony 139

Hubbard, Pearce 153, 157, 159-161,
164

Immigration, Jewish 51, 81, 124, 138,
144, 148

Imperial Airways 71

Italian Convent, Tan Tur 100, 113

Jaffa 55, 88, 90

Jameel 96, 102, 119, 121, 160

Jenny, Sister 100, 137

Jericho 36, 38, 132

Jordan 38
   valley trip 87, 88

Jubillee Day 167

Kerak 115

King David Hotel 123, 124

Kubelik, concert 70

MacInnes, Bishop 27

Malmignati, Count and Countess 86

McLean W.H. 4

Mendelsohn, Mr and Mrs 150

Miller, Miss 97, 110

Mohammed Ali 125

Mount of Olives 9, 12

Nablus 74, 75

Nathanyah 145, 151, 158, 159

Nativity, Church of the 19, 23, 34, 35, 163

Nazareth 46, 128

Nebi Musa 18, 22, 141

Ophel 73

Opthalmic Hospital of the Knights of St John 72, 87

Order of St John of Jerusalem 60

Passover 52

Pension Moscovitz, Tel Aviv 133, 134

Petra, trip to 114-118

Plumer, Lord 54, 83

police 105

population
   Jerusalem 4, 166
   Palestine 124

potteries (revival of) 15, 16

Pringle and Parker (police) 91, 105

Pro-Jerusalem Society 5, 9, 12, 15, 19, 71, 78

Queen Elizabeth (flag ship) 55

Queen of Ethopia 145-147

Ramallah 32

Ramleh 37

Rutenburg
   Mr 160
   scheme 92

riots 18, 96, 101-103, 148, 150

Samuel, Sir Herbert 6, 11, 15, 54

scarlet fever 144

school 97, 110, 153

Scottish Memorial Church 53, 71, 72, 93, 100, 110, 121, 123

Sebastieh 91

smallpox 81

Solomon's
    pools 22, 31, 139
    quarries 28
    stables 66

Sophie 19, 20, 37, 77, 119,

Storrs, Sir Ronald 1, 5, 6, 10, 13, 19, 25, 28, 34, 36, 37, 55, 58, 71, 78

strike, Arab 48

Tabgha (German Hospice) 59, 84

Tan Tur (Italian convent) Tel Aviv 100, 113

Taylor, A.J.P. 1

Tel Aviv 61, 134, 135

Thorndyke, Sybil 131

Tiberias 60, 87, 94

Tombs of the Kings 28

town planning 13, 19, 119

town plans
    Jerusalem 31, 53, 55, 56, 58, 78
    other 78, 94, 145, 153

University, Hebrew 69

Via Dolorosa 64, 89

Virgin Mary, feast of the 65

Wadi Kelt 38, 61, 67

Wailing Wall 18, 93, 101, 105

wall, discovery of remains in Jerusalem 53

water supply 16, 34, 54

Wauchope, Sir Arthur 153, 154, 157

weddings
    Arab 25
    Armenian 48
    Jewish 73

Whiting, Mrs 9

wireless 46, 62, 81

Zionist
    Congress 96
    Movement 81

Zeppelin, Graf 98